TOP 10
WAYS TO
AVOID
TAXES

Praise for
Top 10 Ways to Avoid Taxes

"I finished reading *Top 10 Ways to Avoid TAXES* and had to share my thoughts with you.

"In clear and simple terms, the book lays out some of the most relevant, powerful, and under-utilized approaches to reducing taxes. More importantly, anyone at any income level can use them. Financial literacy is truly lacking in our culture. Those who embrace the principles presented and rely on knowledge-able advisors to direct them can activate the process of truly creating wealth. Thanks for a great resource that I can recommend to my clients."

—*Terry D. Deever, CPA, CFP®, Camarillo, CA*

"The biggest challenge for every tax professional is to explain exceptionally difficult tax concepts to their clients. Mark turns this challenge into a precious life-changing gift in the form of a book. I believe every tax professional should have this book in their office, and of course either recommend it or gift it to their clients.

"Thank you, Mark! You just made our lives easier!"

—*Svetlana Ray, EA, Winnetka, CA*

"Wow, I love this book!

"Once again, Mark Quann opens the eyes of individuals and professionals alike. I enjoyed reading about the tax saving techniques/loopholes and I appreciate the simple down to earth way that Mark describes each strategy. I feel that this book will allow everyone to get a better handle on how to protect their assets and increase their wealth.

"I look forward to advising my clients on these practices and using them personally to protect my own wealth. Thank you Mark for sharing this with the masses!"
—*Maria Shelley, Irvin & Shelley, CPAs, Sherman Oaks, CA*

"You do not have to be an accountant or tax lawyer to understand how to protect yourself from too many taxes. This book gives examples and methods to reduce your tax burden while at the same time benefit financially.

"As a CPA, I provide my clients with various ways to reduce their tax burden, both federal and state taxes. Many of the suggestions that I give my clients are contained within this book. I would recommend this not only to my clients but to anyone who is looking to reduce their tax burden. Sometimes the easiest way to do something is the simplest.

"The information contained in this book will help everyone from the novice taxpayer to the most experienced. The tax code is 77,000 pages. No one knows all the ins and outs of the tax code. Take the time to read this book and find your own buried treasure of tax advice."
—*Quentin Staples, CPA, Woodland Hills, CA*

"No one ever talks about how to make the system work for you. This book tells you how to do just that!

"The Top 10 Ways to Avoid Taxes is more than just a 'how to' book. It's the equivalent of working with a highly specialized team of financial advisors, and for this price?! This book could save you millions of dollars in taxes. If used properly, it is truly a step by step guide to accumulating great wealth."
—*Christina Graves, EA, Owner of Elev8 Tax & Insurance, Bakersfield, CA*

"Mark's first book *Rich Man Poor Bank* was an eye opener for me. I've been giving it away to my clients for many years to help them understand the basics of how money works. They absolutely love it!

"Top 10 Ways to Avoid Taxes takes it one step further. And once again, Mark has found a way to keep it simple and easy to understand. I literally could not put it down! There are so many nuggets about building wealth while at the same time reducing taxes. Anyone who desires to build wealth should read this book!

—*Emily Sang, CPA, Los Angeles, Ca*

"Simple. Informative. Motivational. Mark provides just enough information to not overwhelm yet spurs one to dive into the possibility of achieving great wealth.

It has challenged me to reassess my own plan to implement some of these strategies that I thought were out of my league. I plan to use this book to both educate and encourage my clients to become better stewards of their money. Having a 'can do' attitude is important in all aspects of life and even more so when tackling the bewildering topics of personal finance. This book provides a clear step-by-step roadmap to joining the Top 1%."

—*Palma Mejia, EA, San Pedro, Ca*

"Mark's book provides extremely effective and efficient ways to save money on taxes. It is a practical help to students, professionals, and even the new investor. It is a new way of thinking and making informed decisions. As a finance professor, it helped me to reconsider some financial aspects and adopt different financial approaches. I would recommend this book to all my finance students."

—*Mahdy Elhusseiny, PhD, Professor of Finance, CSUB*

Views and Opinions Disclaimer

This book is presented solely for informational purposes. The author is not offering it as investment, accounting, or other professional services advice. While best efforts have been used in preparing this book, the author makes no representations or warranty of any kind and assumes no liabilities of any kind with respect to the accuracy or completeness of the contents and specifically disclaims any fitness of use for a particular purpose. The author shall not be held liable or responsible to any person or entity with respect to any loss or incidental or consequential damages caused, or alleged to have been caused, directly or indirectly, by the information contained herein.

Every individual's financial situation is different, and the information contained herein may not be suitable for your situation. You should seek the services of a competent professional before beginning any financial program.

Also by Mark J. Quann
Rich Man, Poor Bank

Design and typesetting: Alan Gilbertson, G&G Creative, Los Angeles
Contact alan@gngcreative.com
Front cover design: Iram Shahzadi ("aaniyah.ahmed" 99designs)
Contact irfa6ster@gmail.com

For more information, books, corporate discount plans, media and speaking engagements, email: 10ways@REMiiGroup.com

MARK J. QUANN

TOP 10 WAYS TO AVOID TAXES

with JOSH SHAPIRO

A Guide to WEALTH Accumulation

Before You Read This Book

If you are new to investing, I would highly recommend reading my first book, *Rich Man Poor Bank*. It will give you the basics of how money *really* works. Once you fully understand the basics, you can upgrade to the more advanced financial concepts in this book.

Get a hard copy of this book and buy a highlighter to draw attention to the areas you want to better understand. I believe this book can be a guide to helping you and your family build wealth—avoiding taxes along the way... as much as you legally can, that is.

There is also a **Glossary of Financial Terms** in the back of this book to help you better understand each type of investment. If you encounter a term you don't understand, be sure to go back to the glossary and review the definition. In fact, I would recommend that you read the entire glossary, and define each term before you read the book.

Remember, a financial term is only understood **when you can teach it to others.**

Many of the strategies in this book are not known by 99% of the population.
If you want to join the Top 1%, this book is for you.

Contents

Introduction: Ice Cream & Heart Surgery   1

BUSINESS OWNERSHIP

Tax Avoidance Strategy #1: Business Ownership   13

STOCKS & BONDS

Tax Avoidance Strategy #2: Roth IRA   31

Tax-Avoidance Strategy #3: Municipal Bonds   41

Tax-Avoidance Strategy #4: Capital Gains Taxes   47

Tax-Avoidance Strategy #5: Tax-Loss Harvesting   53

LIFE INSURANCE FOR TAX AVOIDANCE

Tax-Avoidance Strategy #6: The "Rich Man's Roth"   57

REAL ESTATE & "OPM"

Tax-Avoidance Strategy #7: Buy a Home using "OPM" 69

Tax-Avoidance Strategy #8:
$250,000/$500,000 Home Sale Exemption   75

Tax-Avoidance Strategy #9:
Depreciation on Rental Property   83

MORE TAX AVOIDANCE

Tax-Avoidance Strategy #10: "Die!"   89

Tax-Avoidance Strategy #11: "Don't Live in California" 93

ADVANCED WEALTH-BUILDING STRATEGIES

Wealth Accumulation Strategy #1:
A "Principal First" Mortgage   101

Wealth Accumulation Strategy #2:
A Reverse Mortgage to Help You Build Wealth   107

In Conclusion   121

Congratulations!   125

Glossary of Financial Terms   129

Introduction:

Ice Cream & Heart Surgery

(Written from the Intensive Care Unit floor
of USC Keck Hospital)

"**M**Y CPA TOLD ME I WOULD GET A FINE FOR NOT having health insurance," I commented, while talking with my friend Wes.

Wes told me about a faith-based "Health Sharing Plan" which was *not* insurance, but it was a type of reimbursement plan that would pay my medical bills, and I could avoid the penalty for not having insurance. I began my research.

I found out these reimbursement plans do not cover pre-existing conditions, but it was only $150 a month, with a $500 deductible/copay toward any potential medical bills.

"What a great deal…I am never sick anyway, and I could save more money in investments rather than wasting it on an expensive insurance plan."

Like most business owners, I continued to work long hours, keeping my focus on the expansion of the business.

"I'm in perfect health anyway, hiking up mountains on the weekends even in 100-degree weather."

It was late July 2016 when I woke up with a slight pain in my left rib area.

"That's annoying. I'm sure it will go away, eventually."

Finally, into day number three of this chest/rib pain, I mentioned it to my friend Lance.

"You could be having a heart attack, you should go to the emergency room and have it checked out." Lance commented.

"Maybe you're right." And I drove myself to the hospital—located only a couple of miles away from my office. I was admitted right away and they did all sorts of scans, blood tests, and an EKG to determine what was causing my pain.

"Did you know you have a mitral valve prolapse Mr. Quann?" The doctor asked.

"What is that?"

"It is where the valve that pumps blood to your heart is leaking. They sometimes call it a 'leaky valve.'"

"Is it dangerous?"

"It depends. If it gets worse, it could cause you some problems in the future. You will need to have it monitored. Our tests showed no indication of a heart attack, and you seem to be healthy. We can't find any reason for the chest pain, so we are referring you to a cardiologist."

"I've seen it many times Mr. Quann," commented the cardiologist. "It is just an infection in your ribs, and it should go away in a couple of days. You don't even need any medication."

"That is great news, but what do I do about the mitral valve prolapse?"

"Don't worry about it too much. Like I said, many people have a mitral valve prolapse and don't know about it their entire lives. It may never affect your health."

I was relieved, and thanked the doctor for his time.

Later, when returning from Hawaii in mid-February 2018, I felt very sick, with major congestion and shortness of breath. After being admitted (again) to the emergency room, I did not receive good news at all. I was diagnosed with "atrial fibrillation." I was told that tests had shown that my "leaky valve" had gotten much worse, and my heart was no longer pumping in a normal rhythm.

"Well Mark, atrial fibrillation causes the heart to pulsate rather than pump. Between your valve not pumping enough blood to your heart, and your heart pulsating, your body is suffocating from lack of oxygen. I'm afraid you will need open heart surgery. We will have to run some more tests, but we will try to get you booked for the surgery in the next couple of days."

We then began discussing the options for the different types of valves available, if "valve replacement" was necessary.

"Your first option is a mechanical valve made of titanium. It will last the rest of your life, but the valve increases the risk of blood clots, which can cause a stroke. To reduce that risk, you will have to take a blood thinner called Coumadin (Warfarin) for the rest of your life."

"Doc, I don't want to be on Coumadin for life. What are my options?"

"The other option is to use a pig's valve. You will only have to take Coumadin for a couple of months, but you will need to come back every five to seven years for another valve replacement."

I thanked the doctor for his time, and sat alone in my hospital room, hooked up to needles in both arms, and oxygen to help me breathe. Throughout the night it seemed like a nurse would arrive every few hours for more tests. As they arrived to make an injection into my stomach, I remember feeling very scared.

"Mark, I've got some morphine for the pain, this should put you right to sleep."

Before long, my eyelids began to feel heavy, and I began to have the most random thoughts:

"I can't believe I need open heart surgery at age 40."

"Will my health sharing plan cover the cost of the surgery?"

"At least I have 2.8 million in life insurance that I bought before I got sick."

"What am I going to do with all this downtime?"

"Should I write another book?"

That was my final thought before I went to sleep.

That next morning, while chatting with a hospital nurse, I found out she had worked at many different hospitals in Southern California. She had seen the results of *all* types of heart surgeries.

"Mark I could lose my job for telling you this, but whatever they recommend for you here, go and get a second opinion."

I was shocked. I did not know what to say…

Did a complete stranger risk losing her job to warn me that they don't offer the *best* options for my surgery *in this hospital?*

Why would she do that?

After she finished some more tests, I thanked her for the time she spent with me, and assured her that I wouldn't mention our conversation.

That next day, I spent most of the day researching the alternative options to having open heart surgery. I learned about "minimally invasive"—where they don't cut your chest open and move your ribs to expose your heart, but only make two incisions to complete the surgery. It was a much shorter recovery time, with much less pain. I also learned about "robotic"—where they fix your heart and valve using "robot arms" to assist in the surgery.

In speaking with that same nurse that next day (I'll refer to her as "My Hero Nurse" from here on in), I asked her,

"Who *is* the best?"

Without delay, she replied, "Doctor Mark Cunningham at USC. People travel from all around the world to have their surgery done with him."

I had no idea how, but I decided that I was going to leave this hospital, and I would get my surgery done with Dr. Cunningham.

Before leaving the hospital that next day, I was given more bad news:

"Mr. Quann, I want you to be very aware that once you leave the hospital, it is not likely they will admit you back because you have no health insurance. The only reason we had booked you for surgery is because you arrived in our emergency room, and by law we cannot turn you away. Once you leave, you may find that no hospital will admit you for surgery. Be sure you are making the right decision before you leave."

Shortly after, I called several hospitals and verified they would not book me for surgery unless I had health insurance.

Upon my release, I spoke with several doctors and administrators of the hospital.

"Mr. Quann, we will release you, but you need to get this surgery done as soon as possible. We are prescribing four medications. You will need to take them two times a day, to control your blood pressure and to keep you from having a stroke, and to help keep your heart pumping properly."

I signed the release forms and left the hospital.

Over the next month, I did a tremendous amount of research while also trying to work. I had limited energy, I was feeling sick most of the time, and just walking up a flight of stairs I found myself gasping for air.

I continued calling numerous hospitals, verifying that no hospital will book my surgery without proof of insurance.

I certainly would not have access to the best hospitals and surgeons without having a great health insurance plan.

I was sick, and getting worse, and my options were not good.

Only when consulting with my friend Lance, did he tell me of a possible option.

"You have a business, a corporation, and an employee, right?"

"Yes, that's right."

"I believe you can purchase a group health insurance plan. It would cover preexisting conditions, and your corporation can buy it any time of year—not just during open enrollment like regular health insurance."

I immediately began the application for a group health insurance plan.

Although my health insurance was not yet approved, I had a chance to meet with Dr. Cunningham. We talked for over an hour and a half. He answered all my questions and fully educated me on the different types of surgeries—from open heart, to robotic, and minimally invasive. He told me of the results he had gotten in the past eighteen years of doing *all* types of surgeries. I could tell Dr. Cunningham had a passion for what he did, and he truly cared for every one of his patients.

"After reviewing your records, I don't believe you will need valve replacement," said Dr. Cunningham. "I also believe I can get your heart out of atrial fibrillation (back to a normal rhythm) using a procedure called 'maze procedure.' If everything goes well, you could live a normal and active lifestyle, without being on drugs, or having to need another valve replacement."

He then educated me about the potential risks of having *any* type of heart surgery.

"Mr. Quann, because we have to stop your heart and hook you up to a bypass machine, I must let you know that there is a long list of bad things that can happen during, and after the surgery. Would you like a copy of that list?"

I laughed. "No thanks Doc," and I left his office.

On April 20th, I was admitted to USC Keck Medical Center for minimally invasive heart and valve repair. The surgery went well. My valve was fixed, and for the first time in months, my heart was beating normally. Even though I was in a lot of pain, I could finally breathe properly again.

What I will never forget is what happened to me before being released from USC.

While in my room, I was talking to one of the nurses and I noticed she had a very similar accent to My Hero Nurse. I wondered if they knew each other. I mentioned her name.

She had a big smile, "Oh, yes, I've known her for over ten years, she is like a sister to me. She is also working tonight in the hospital."

I told her the story of how I ended up at USC, and that I needed to say thank you. She smiled, and called My Hero Nurse to my room. After only a few minutes, she arrived.

Immediately upon walking into my room, she recognized me. She had a big smile, and was very happy to see me. I gave her a hug as tears ran down from my eyes.

I finally got to ask her, *"Why did you risk your job to help me?"*

"Mark, you are a young man and I didn't care, I wanted to make sure you researched all the options for your heart surgery. Somehow, I knew you would make it to USC. I had also been wondering what happened to you."

We talked for quite some time. Before she left, she told me, "Mark, you made my day."

I sat in my hospital room that night eating a bowl of ice cream. I found myself thinking of all the miracles that had to happen for me to be there. In speaking with many of the staff in the hospital, most from other countries, they told me how lucky I was to get my surgery done in *this* hospital, with *this* doctor.

At age forty, I have always learned the best life-lessons come when times are the hardest, not in the best of times.

I began to reflect, and wrote down the lessons I had learned:

Always do a lot of research, and ask a lot of questions when buying any financial or insurance product: Being a financial expert myself, I did not ask the right questions and had purchased the wrong type of health insurance plan. It almost cost me my life.

Be friendly, and treat everyone with importance: If I had not been friendly with My Hero Nurse, I doubt she would have stuck her neck out to help me.

Ice cream is like heart surgery: There are many flavors, and many shops to buy ice cream. The same is true for heart surgery. If you end up in the wrong ice cream shop, you'll be okay. But if you end up in the wrong hospital—where they only offer one "flavor" of heart surgery—it could be devastating to your future.

Money buys better options: The reason I'm so passionate about making financial education available to everyone, is that money has bought me *better options* in my life.

It is true that money won't buy you happiness, but it can buy your children a better education, better food, the best insurance plans, better homes in better neighborhoods, better cars and better vacations. It can even buy you better advice on investments and tax avoidance—which in turn can buy you better ice cream…and more of all of the above.

And perhaps, one day, God forbid, money will also buy you the best surgeon in the best hospital in the world for your heart surgery.

Then, *it* happened.

The question I had asked myself many months ago popped in my head.

What will I do with all this downtime?

I recalled my final thought before I went to sleep... *Should I write another book?*

It was right then that I decided to write *this* book.

As crazy as it sounds, the reason for this book, and the inspiration behind it, is *because* I had heart surgery. It would not exist today without it.

But...what will I write about?

I then asked myself another question. *What is it that most of my clients complain about as they make more money?*

The answer was clear: Taxes!

I should write a book about all the strategies that I use to avoid taxes!

While sitting in that hospital bed, I found myself both excited and inspired. I pulled out my laptop and began typing away.

I've always wanted to be wealthy—mainly because wealth opens the door to better options. If you would like the *best* options in life, for you and your family, you too will also need to pursue WEALTH.

To get wealthy, you will need a world class financial education...with an "MBA" in avoiding taxes—your *largest* obstacle to building wealth.

~

Although this is a short book, I don't recommend reading it in one sitting. Only read one chapter a day. Then try to explain each tax avoidance strategy to a friend or family member.

⁓

Just because you read it, doesn't mean you understand it. You only truly understand something when you can teach it to others.

PART ONE

BUSINESS OWNERSHIP

"You can't be for big government, big taxes, and big bureaucracy, and still be for the little guy."
—Ronald Reagan

CHAPTER ONE

Tax Avoidance Strategy #1:
Business Ownership

B EFORE WE COVER HOW BUSINESS OWNERSHIP CAN help you avoid taxes, I think it is important that you learn where tax rates have been, and more importantly, where they may go in the future.

I also think it is important to learn how the government has built a system where many unsuspecting Americans will get hammered in taxes in the future. Of course, we will also cover how you can avoid many of these taxes—with business ownership being the most important of all the tax avoidance strategies.

Benjamin Franklin is quoted as saying, "The only thing certain is 'death' and 'taxes'."

That is true. Well, sort of.

Death is 100% certain for us all, but how *certain* are taxes?

Let's first simplify taxes:

"When you earn it... they tax it."

"When you save it... they tax it."

"When you spend it... they tax it."

"And when you die... guess what happens. Yup, they tax that too!"

If you have read *Rich Man Poor Bank,* you learned that the banking cartels keep the general population ignorant of how money *actually* works. Today, everyone, regardless of income, is taught: "Saving money and getting good credit will lead to your financial freedom." Nothing is further from the truth. Saving money in a bank, and getting good credit, only makes *bankers* wealthy.

The entirety of this book could be summarized in the following:

The poor and middle class teach their kids:

» How to get a job
» How to save money
» How to get good credit
» And... "Pay your taxes"

The rich teach their kids:

» How to run a business
» How to invest
» And... How to *avoid* taxes

I believe the above statements are what separate the rich from the poor, and why the rich continue to get richer and the poor continue to get poorer.

Just like the biggest banks, big government will increase their tax revenue *if* the masses don't understand the many ways to reduce and avoid taxes. As long as our schools are funded by debt and taxes, there will never be a class called "How to Avoid Debt & Taxes - 101."

The good news is, that when you raise your financial IQ, the amount you would pay in interest to the banks, and the amount you would pay in taxes can be dramatically reduced.

Your goal should be to obtain what I call a "Rich Man Education." A "Rich Man Education" is learning how running a business can help you avoid taxes.

You should also learn tax reduction strategies when investing in all different types of investments—including stocks and bonds, mutual funds, Exchange Traded Funds (ETF's), and real estate. Lastly, you should learn how and why the rich, and the banks, invest inside life insurance policies to avoid taxes. We will cover that later in Chapter 6.

With a "Rich Man Education" you will understand the risks and rewards of each type of investment, and whenever possible, how to reduce taxes. In some cases, we can show you how to not pay any taxes on *all* your profit.

To understand tax avoidance, you must first learn the different *types* of taxes.

But before we go through a few of the most common types, I want you to ask yourself a question:

"Do I think it is possible, that in the future, the government will tax my income at 60%-70%?"

Did you answer yes? Or no? Seriously…stop, and think about this.

If your answer is no, then I would encourage you to open the history book of tax rates. After the Great Depression, in the 1940's, you will find that the highest federal tax rate for those with a "high income," was 94%!

Yes, 94%!

Then you *still* had to pay taxes to the state you lived in. If your state taxes were 2%, the government was taking 96% of your income.

This is the reason why actor-soon-turned politician, and eventually President of the United States, Ronald Reagan only made two movies a year. For any additional movies made that year, *all* of his income would go to taxes.

Once he became President, he realized that when taxes were too high, many of the most productive people were deterred from working harder to earn more money. In 1981, Reagan significantly reduced the maximum tax rate, which affected the highest income earners and lowered the top marginal tax rate from 70% to 50%; in 1986 he further reduced the tax rate to 28%.

It should be noted that back in the 70's the government had fewer types of taxes than today—however, the tax rates were higher.

Today, we have both high taxes *and* hundreds of different types of taxes—yet a limited number of ways to avoid them.

And when the government can't raise taxes, they employ a new strategy: *Theft!*

That being such a controversial statement, I'm assuming you would like me to provide an example of how the government steals from the American people.

Okay, here you go:

I think you would find it interesting that social security—specifically the payments that would be sent to you in retirement—used to *always* arrive in your account tax-free.

The crafty politicians, always looking for ways to create more tax revenue, decided that the Social Security Trust Fund would be an easy target. And because *reducing* social security payments would be unpopular for voters, they decided to take another approach.

In 1983, rather than reduce social security payments, they began taxing those payments; the same result as reducing them. Aka "theft."

If a private company employed this type of strategy, someone would end up in jail. But when you are the government—and you make the rules—you can change them anytime you want.

"Do these taxes apply to everyone?" you ask.

Nope!

They only apply to those that earn income in retirement just above "middle class." They also don't apply to those that know how *to avoid all the taxes* on social security payments—regardless of the amount of income they receive.

The formula is simple: It is understanding what *types* of income will cause taxation of your social security, and avoid those types of income. This is called "Provisional Income," which is the formula the IRS uses to determine what types of income will cause your social security benefits to be taxed. We will also cover this later in Chapter 6.

Now, let's cover the most common types of taxes, and more importantly, how to avoid paying the highest rates.

There are:

Federal income taxes, state income taxes, city taxes, capital gains taxes, property taxes, self-employment taxes, alternative minimum taxes (AMTs), sales taxes, gasoline taxes, hotel taxes, auto registration taxes, water taxes, electricity taxes, cell phone taxes, and the list goes on and on.

There is even a "sin tax," taxing things such as alcohol and cigarettes. And, in the coming years, the government will continue to create more taxes—taxes when you earn, save, invest, and spend your money. And yes, more taxes when you die.

The rich understand that income taxes, both federal and state, are the highest forms of all taxes. So rather than focus on making more money from a job, they focus on earning more money *from sources other than a job*.

The first and most important step to avoiding taxes is:

Step 1: Business Ownership

If you study taxes, as I have done for over a decade, you will learn that the government taxes heavily those things it does not want us to do. For example, the "sin tax" is applied to tobacco and alcohol to raise the price, in the hopes it will deter teens from smoking and drinking.

Conversely, the government rewards, with reduced taxes, the things it wants to see more of. For example: When you donate money to charity, that helps the charity. And, in turn, hopefully helps those in poverty—thus reducing the burden to the government to take care of them.

Another example: When you invest in stocks or bonds, it helps businesses expand, helps the economy, and in turn creates more jobs—again, providing more tax revenue for the government.

The government also wants to reward business ownership: When businesses grow, they provide more jobs, expand the economy, and again, raise more tax revenue.

If you already own a business, you likely know the basics for maximizing your tax deductions, and you already have a tax professional to help guide you.

If you don't have a business, then you will need to find a way to start one, either part time or full time.

There was a time that I did not own a business. I had never sold anything. I didn't know what the phrase "tax deduction" meant. But I chose to invest heavily in my financial education, reading books and going to seminars to learn everything I could. I continue to do so to this day to raise my financial IQ, gain financial and business skills, improve and change my habits, and yes, become a master at legally avoiding taxes.

Now, there are many types of businesses to own. But since this is not a book on "The advantages of different business models," I would rather focus on the *skills* needed to own any successful business.

The most valuable skills are:

» People skills
» Sales skills
» Money skills
» Money habits

As you decide to start a business, start investing in yourself to improve your people skills, sales skills, and money skills. And when you make more money, you will want to improve your money habits.

It is unfortunate we don't teach "How to Start a Business" in school.

People Skills

I would recommend a book called "How to Win Friends and Influence People" by Dale Carnegie. Once you read this book, practice using your newfound "people skills" with your family, friends and coworkers. Watch the *"magic"* happen around you, as people begin to like and trust you even more, and will be more willing to help you.

Your people skills will be used every day regardless of the business you are in, and will be the key to your financial success. As I mentioned in the Introduction, just by being friendly and listening to My Hero Nurse, she risked losing her job to help me. I don't think she would have done so without me studying people skills, and learning to be more likable by all types of people.

What you will learn is that people will only open doors for you *if* they like you, and trust you.

Over the years, many doors have been opened for me, and countless opportunities have been presented to me only because I've earned the trust of people.

I would go so far to say that, in the many years I have spent in business, the most valuable skill I have learned is working with and understanding people.

It is unfortunate we don't teach "People Skills" in school.

Sales Skills

Learning to *sell* was scary and intimidating to me. I was the son of a bricklayer. I never had to *sell* anything before. But a mentor and wealthy friend of mine once told me, "Learning to sell can be challenging and uncomfortable. But not learning to sell may leave you struggling financially for the rest of your life—which is much more 'challenging and uncomfortable'?"

Thirteen years ago, I sucked it up, entered the financial services industry and learned all I could. I eventually learned to sell, and with that came freedom, and yes, better choices. Fortunately, today, I don't consider what I do as "sales," as I would rather simply educate you—the reader. Then you can decide for yourself what tax avoidance strategies work best for you and make better-informed financial decisions.

My advice today is that before you start a business, go work for a company that will pay you a salary plus bonuses based on your sales. Many companies have great training programs on "how to sell," and with that skill you are much more likely to become successful in *any* business.

It is unfortunate we don't teach "Sales Skills" in school.

Money Skills

This is fully understanding the *fundamentals* of money, and all the ways that you can put money to work for you. This is also understanding all ten ways to avoid taxes, and how to move your money from one investment strategy to another—many times not paying any taxes at all.

For example: You will learn how to invest your after-tax money—made from your business, which reduced the amount of taxes you paid when earning it—and invest and grow it in one tax-free strategy, and then move it to another strategy...all without paying taxes.

The "Ultimate Money Skill" is this:

Reduce taxes when you earn your money,

Pay no taxes on the growth of your money,

Pay no taxes when you spend your money,

Pass that wealth to your heirs 100% tax-free.

Of course, this is all done using legal IRS tax codes that are all well known by the wealthiest people in America.

And with such a strong statement above on tax-avoidance, I think it is about time for another important disclosure:

Mark Quann and his books do not provide tax, legal or accounting advice. This material has been prepared for informational purposes only, and is not intended to provide, and should not be relied on for, tax, legal or accounting advice. You should consult with your own tax, legal and accounting advisors before engaging in the buying or selling of any investment.

It is unfortunate we don't teach "Money Skills" in school.

Money Habits

Money Habits are simply the habits you have with your money, which will determine what you do with it *after* you have earned it.

This is controlling your *emotions* when it comes to your money—and making the best financial decisions, not emotional ones. This is also where having good advisors is priceless, as they can help you make non-emotional financial decisions.

This is also making a choice to surround yourself with other business owners and entrepreneurs, and to learn from each other at every opportunity.

Remember this:

Choosing *who* you spend your time with and guarding your associations is very important *if* you are serious about becoming wealthy. "Show me your friends and I'll show you your future" has taught me to hang around others that own businesses, have good money skills, good money habits, and who also understand (and love) tax-avoidance.

It is unfortunate we don't teach "The Money Habits Needed to get Wealthy" in school.

Business Owners Pay Less Tax

Let me quickly give you the basics of why business owners pays less in taxes than employees. Once you own a business, a number of expenses can be deducted from your income, *if* the money is spent during the course of running your business.

22

Here are a few examples:

» Computers
» The cost of Internet
» The cost of your cell phone, if used for your business
» A portion of your cell phone bill, the portion used for business
» A mileage deduction when driving your car
» The cost of health insurance
» Licensing costs
» Office rent
» If you're using a portion of your home for business, you can take a business deduction, *if* it is used "regularly" and "exclusively" for business. This deduction could be significant, for example, if running a daycare out of your home.
» Paying the babysitter, but only when volunteering at a recognized charity or not-for-profit. (Volunteering is a great way to help others, while also making business contacts.)
» Buying books that teach business, sales, or other skills needed to run a business
» If inviting prospects clients and employees to a company BBQ, the food, alcohol and other costs can be a deduction from your income.

Even a trip to Hawaii can become a business deduction under certain circumstances. Let me explain: If in the course of your business you ran a sales competition, and the top salespeople won a trip to Hawaii, the cost of that vacation for you and those employees can be a deduction.

Once your income rises, you won't want to pay the high cost of self-employment taxes, about 13%. Your next step is to talk with your tax advisor who can advise you when it is time to set your business up as a corporation. An "S-Corporation" is the most common type of corporation used by small business owners. This can help you reduce taxes even further, as corporations don't pay self-employment taxes.

Finally, a SEP IRA can be funded to reduce your taxes and save for retirement. But, I think it is important to note: I don't use or generally suggest a SEP IRA, as I don't believe in "saving money on the seed to pay taxes on the harvest." (Covered in detail in the following chapters).

Those are only some of the most common ways to reduce your taxes when owning a business.

Your next step is to know how to keep and manage the money that you earn.

Step 2: Manage Your Money

I've seen dozens of businesses crash and burn because the owner was mismanaging their *personal* finances when times were good, but with one economic downturn, they lost all their "stuff"— their home, then came the divorce, and the loss of their business too.

Great investors are careful about their spending. They like to have lots of different types of investments for short, mid, and long-term investing, and they know how each are taxed (or not taxed).

The rich also like to keep lots of liquidity in order to move their money to other more profitable investments, whenever they see an opportunity.

The rich drive regular cars when building their wealth, and are not looking to impress anyone with a fancy car. They are not trying to "keep up with the Joneses" ...buying fancy cars and watches *before* they are wealthy.

You must look at yourself: Are you a "spender"? Do you spend everything you earn?

What was your answer? Yes? Or no? It is important for you to recognize if you are, as the first step to recovery is to recognize you have a problem.

Or, are you an "investor"? Do you prioritize investing *first*, and then spend only *after* you have invested?

Invest!

Below is the order of how the most successful business owners in the world prioritize their investing:

The best return on investment (ROI) will always be investing into yourself—reading books and studying to upgrade your skills.

Your second best investment is to invest back into your business; whether it is getting another license, paying someone to do part-time marketing for you, training an employee, or paying an accountant to help explain tax avoidance.

Depending on your business, you may even want to invest the time, energy, and money into writing a book. My first book took five years, but this book took only thirty days, writing just a few hours a day while recovering from heart surgery.

Your third investment should be investing a *minimum* of ten percent of your income back into the tax-advantaged investments covered in the following chapters.

Another very important aspect of becoming wealthy is "giving back." If you study the richest men in history, they all made it a priority to donate ten percent of their income, giving to church or charity. In many ways they believed that this was the most important "investment."

25

Step 3: Pay Yourself First

Step three is known as "Paying Yourself First." But I believe that all four steps are equally important. You *always* invest first, and then you can spend whatever is left.

Whether you are an employee or a business owner, you will need to "Pay Yourself First," and know how to shelter your after-tax money from further taxes. "After-tax money" is the money you have earned and paid your taxes on—and it likely sits lazy in your checking or savings account.

What the banks don't want you to know about is what they do with your money while it sits lazy in your account. When you close your eyes at night to sleep, all the money in the mega-banks is "swept" somewhere else—where it earns money for the banks.

These mega-banks and corporations use these "sweep accounts"—also called "Zero Balance Accounts" (ZBAs)—to put *your* money hard at work for them rather than you. We will cover in Chapter 12 how to use this "sweep" feature to help *you* rather than your bank.

Summary

To close out this chapter, let's summarize:

You need to have some sort of business to reduce taxes when you *earn* your money.

You will need to learn people skills, sales skills and money skills to have a successful business, and develop good money habits.

Your business can also help reduce taxes when you *spend* your money.

Everyone, business owner or not, will have after-tax money sitting lazy in checking and savings accounts. Here is what I have found after 19 years of studying money: It is important to put all your money, including your lazy money, hard at work for you. The right strategies can help you avoid taxes when you *save and invest* your money.

Lastly, not a topic covered in this chapter, but you also need to eliminate taxes when you *die.*

As we travel down the curvy and rugged road of wealth-accumulation, one day, with a great amount of persistence, you may join the ranks of "The Wealthy."

Here is the secret that only the wealthy know: Tax avoidance becomes *easier* as your wealth increases.

Later in this book we will cover how to use "Other People's Money" (OPM) to supercharge several wealth accumulation strategies.

The rest of this book will focus on investing and tax avoidance, using the after-tax money from your job or business.

If you would like to start a business teaching others tax avoidance,
text "Opportunity" to: (833) 455-4540
or Email: 10ways@REMiiGroup.com

PART TWO

STOCKS & BONDS

"A fine is a tax for doing something wrong. A tax is a fine for doing something right."
—Anonymous

CHAPTER TWO

Tax Avoidance Strategy #2:
Roth IRA

MOTIVATIONAL SPEAKER, BUSINESSMAN, AND self-help author Jim Rohn is quoted as saying, *"Profits are better than wages."*
Jim was a genius for his ability to teach others and keep it simple and easy to understand. Jim has been a mentor of mine for many years, and I know Jim was right. Profits are better than wages—as profits are unlimited, and they are taxed less than wages.

But here is what I will teach my children one day:

"Profits are better than wages, but tax-free profits are my favorite kind."

Let me tell you the Story of Four Brothers to help you better understand tax avoidance.

Four brothers, **A**lbert, **B**rian, **C**harlie and **D**anny, all decided they wanted to become financially free. They lived in different cities, had different friends, and access to many opinions about money.

Having never been educated about money in school, they all began asking friends and relatives for advice.

All four brothers were in their early to mid 20's and had the same plan:

» Save $5000 a year toward retirement
» Invest for forty years
» Pass on a family legacy

—

The first brother, Albert, consulted with his good friend Sam:

Sam worked for one of the mega-banks and told Albert, "I have great news for you. We have a special this month called a 'Super Saver High Yield' savings account. It will grow every single year guaranteed. And when the market crashes, you won't lose any money. We can start up an automatic-saver program for you, for $417 a month. Start saving now and watch your account grow larger each year."

"That sounds great Sam, because I don't want to lose any money."

They finished the paperwork, and Albert left the bank.

—

The second brother, Brian, spoke to his Aunt Janice. Aunt Janice gave him some different advice:

"A Roth IRA can help you avoid taxes on your money. Like a farmer, 'you'll pay taxes on the seed, so you won't be taxed on the harvest.' It grows without any taxes on the gains each year, and all your retirement money can be accessed tax-free."

"That sounds great, no taxes!"

His aunt, a very conservative investor, had Certificates of Deposit (most commonly known as CDs) at her local bank.

"They are guaranteed not to lose any money, and when investing in a CD, you will earn a higher rate than a savings account," Aunt Janice exclaimed.

She introduced Brian to her friend Vanessa at the bank. Vanessa set up an automatic savings program for $417 a month into a "Magic Flex Roth IRA CD."

The third brother, Charlie, spoke to his accountant:

"Be smart. Invest into stocks and don't worry if the market goes up or down—just keep investing. If the market crashes, you will be buying shares of stock on sale, and accumulating more shares of those companies at cheaper prices. You will 'buy low to later sell high.'

"We can set it up as an IRA so you save taxes now. You will likely be in a lower tax bracket in your retirement years, so an IRA makes sense."

Charlie opened an IRA investing $417 a month into the S&P 500 - the 500 biggest stocks in the US, sometimes called an "Index fund."

The fourth brother, Danny, spoke with his friend Sandra. Sandra had invested into books and seminars to educate herself about how money works, and gave very different advice:

"Danny, I think you should open a Roth IRA and invest into a 100% stock portfolio. Since you have 40 years to invest, don't be conservative and invest every month—regardless if the market is going up or down. You can use a Mutual Fund or an Exchange Traded Fund to diversify your investments, and reduce the risk. Invest for the long-hall, knowing you will have a bunch of tax-free cash to spend when you decide to retire. And here is the coolest part about a Roth IRA: all the distributions are tax-free! You also can collect your social security tax-free as well—as Roth IRA distributions do not cause taxation of your social security benefits.

"Providing the government doesn't change the rules, and social security is still around, that is 100% tax-free retirement!"

Danny opened his Roth IRA and invested $417 a month.

⌒

All four Brothers had invested a total of $200,000 over 40 years.

"Were the results that different?"

Well, you tell me:

⌒

Albert accumulated a total of $268,000 in his "Super Saver High Yield" savings account for his retirement.

This would generate $5,000 each year "guaranteed."

However, after accounting for inflation, Albert would only be retiring on about $1250 a year in today's dollars.

Albert would live in poverty, even with his tax-free social security payments. He would have to supplement his income working at McDonald's—and his arthritis pain would make it difficult to work. On a positive note, at least Albert had free food while working as a "McSenior."

⌒

Brian accumulated a total of $387,000 in his "Magic Flex Roth IRA CD" for his retirement.

He would receive about $16,000 each year, tax-free.

However, after accounting for inflation, Brian would only be retiring on about $4000 a year in today's dollars.

Brian, similar to Albert, would also retire in poverty, even with his tax-free social security payments. At age 67, Brian would have to get a job as a Walmart greeter to supplement his income—and take advantage of his "employee discounts" to save money on groceries and clothing.

⌒

Charlie accumulated a total of $2,675,000 in his IRA, because he had invested into stocks.

He would receive $160,000 each year. But he forgot that he would have to now pay taxes on his money. He hadn't in fact arrived in retirement in a lower tax bracket as he had thought. After paying Uncle Sam his taxes, this left him with only $120,000 a year.

However, after accounting for inflation, Charlie would only be retiring on about $30,000 a year in today's dollars.

Soon, Charlie got some bad news in the mail.

He learned that his IRA distributions (as opposed to a Roth IRA) caused his social security payments to be taxable, further eating into his retirement income. Charlie, after 40 years of investing, had very little extra income. There would be no lavish vacations as he had envisioned. He had arrived in his Golden Years as a "millionaire," only to live a life in the lower-middle class.

Then, Charlie got some more bad news in the mail.

At age 70½, Uncle Sam sent him a letter. After being translated from mumbo-jumbo into English, it said something like this:

"Dear Charlie,

"Over the past 40 years you have not paid us any taxes on the money you invested into your IRA, so you need to start taking distributions now, called 'Required Minimum Distributions,' or 'RMD's.' You see, we have been waiting a long time for this. We have a lot of big government pensions that need to be funded in Washington, and it is time to collect some taxes.

"At least you have the satisfaction, when sleeping at night, knowing that your tax dollars are being spent to help other hard-working Americans retire.

*"Oh yes, we have also enclosed a handy-dandy schedule to show you how much money you **must** remove each year from your retirement account. If you don't take it out as we say, we will take a 50% penalty first, and then collect our taxes.*

"Enjoy your retirement!

"Sincerely, Uncle Sam"

After reviewing the schedule of annual RMD's, Charlie would be forced to take out more and more money each year from his IRA. But not only would Charlie have to take out his income each year, he would be forced to spend-down his retirement account even faster—and pay even more taxes at those ever-increasing tax rates.

Then, Charlie got *even more* bad news in the mail.

Again, after being translated from mumbo-jumbo into English, it said something like this:

"Dear Charlie,

"We know what a proud and patriotic American you are, and how you love to help your fellow Americans. We want to help you to help all the 10's of millions of Americans that didn't save for retirement.

"Simply stated, with your millions in your retirement account: congratulations! You have become one of 'The Wealthy' and need to pay your fair share.

"After a slight increase in tax rates, here is what you can expect to pay in taxes on your retirement income:

"55% for Federal Taxes, plus 15% for State Taxes.

"Enjoy your retirement!

"Sincerely, Uncle Sam"

Within a few years of increased income—caused by his RMD's—and rising tax rates, Charlie was now part of those

"High Income Earners" and would pay 70% of his income each year back to Uncle Sam.

Are you enjoying the Story of our Four Brothers so far?

Let's read-on to see how Danny did.

⌣

Danny also accumulated $2,675,000 for his retirement, just like Charlie did. But Danny used a Roth IRA as opposed to a regular IRA, thereby making his account 100% tax-free.

He would receive $160,000 a year from his account, and no taxes would be due.

After accounting for inflation, Danny would be retiring on about $40,000 a year in today's dollars.

Fortunately for Danny, not only would his Roth IRA payments be tax-free, but they also would not cause taxation of his social security payments. He would enjoy his social security tax-fee, and use it to supplement his tropical island getaways.

Finally, because Danny had used a Roth IRA, there would never be any RMD's.

So Danny never got a letter in the mail.

Danny's $2.67 million would always be free of taxes. And without those forced distributions, Danny had the option of passing more tax-free money to his heirs.

⌣

Yes, quite a difference indeed!

"Well, what exactly is a Roth IRA, and how does it work?" you ask.

Here are the basics:

A Roth IRA was created in 1997 from Senator William Roth. Senator Roth wanted to encourage saving for retirement, and gave Americans the option of building tax-free retirement income.

» A Roth IRA must be funded with after-tax money.
» The money grows without any taxes.
» The income received at retirement age is exempt from all taxes.
» The income also does not trigger taxation of your social security benefits.
» The maximum amount you can currently deposit is $5500 per year. (It was only $2000 per year in 1997 and has stepped up gradually over the years.)
» If you have a job, you may have the option from your employer to contribute to a "Roth 401(k)" plan and have higher maximum contribution limits.
» If your income is "too high" you can be phased out from making Roth IRA contributions. Therefore, it doesn't work for mid to high income earners. (We will cover the "Rich Man's Roth" in chapter 6.)

—

Although Roth IRA's are good for many people, I must confess: I don't have a Roth IRA. And I'll likely never fund one.

You'll understand why as you read on and learn of the more sophisticated strategies that can be used to build wealth.

What I don't like about Roth IRA's are:

» Roth IRA's don't provide "leverage," or "Other People's Money"—the key to wealth accumulation.
» A Roth IRA will generally crash in an economic downturn. I would rather make money when the markets rise, but not lose any when the markets crash. I also would rather buy in after the crash when stocks are undervalued, or "cheap." This will also be covered in Chapter 6.

» And finally, I can't access all my cash prior to age 59½ if it is within a Roth IRA. Not to brag, but my retirement age is forty! "Retirement" is not an age—it is a net worth. Today, my business allows me to work when I want, on what I enjoy, and earn as much money as I want.

Does that sound better than retiring at age 65? Yes, I thought so.

In the next chapter we will cover why municipal bonds can be a useful tool to put some of your lazy money to work for you, while avoiding taxes and always having "liquidity"— meaning you can access your cash quickly and easily.

"All taxes discourage something.
Why not discourage bad things like
pollution rather than good things like
working or investment?"
—Lawrence Summers
Chief Economist of the World Bank

CHAPTER THREE

Tax-Avoidance Strategy #3:
Municipal Bonds

I N SCHOOL THEY TEACH LOTS OF STUFF, LIKE "THE THREE
R's": **R**eading, w**R**iting, and a**R**ithmetic.

They also teach history, physical education and science.
When the students graduate to attend college or university,
the first classes are "How to fill out your application for student loans" and, "How to get your first credit card—to help
you build your credit."

After 4 years, these students leave school hoping to find
a good job, and only then learn how crippling the payments
are on their student loans. They also learn that these loans
will never go away for the rest of their lives until paid in full.

The teachers are overworked and underpaid, and many
struggle their entire lives because they never got a financial
education—despite the fancy diplomas on their walls.

On the other hand, the mega-banks get to lend billions of
dollars to these unsuspecting students, pushing them heavily
into debt before they even make their first paycheck. The
mega-banks get to borrow at super low interest rates, then
lend it back to the students at much higher interest rates—

with a guarantee that the student can never default. Not even bankruptcy will set them free.

And when I talk to these new graduates and ask them a basic financial question such as, "What is a municipal bond?" they simply don't know.

If they do happen to find a good paying job, only then do they learn of an oppressive tax system that will take forty to fifty percent of their income because they rise above the average.

If you were to ask them, "Can you name three ways to invest without taxes?" almost none are able to do it.

What worries me most is that I've not found a single school that teaches any real financial education. And if they tried to put together a curriculum to teach kids about money, under the heels of the bankers, they would continue to teach "How to save money, and how to get good credit."

For this reason, I believe that the top 1% must carry the burden to educate the 99% about how money works—specifically: how to reduce taxes through business ownership, how to invest without taxes, how to retire tax-free, and how to pass that money to their heirs, also tax-free.

Both this book and my first book, Rich Man Poor Bank, are attempts to "level the playing field" as they say, so you too can have an opportunity to join the top 1%. You know what they say… "If you can't beat em, join em."

And when you join the top 1%, armed with a world-class financial education and your money working hard for you, in time, you may even join the ranks of the top 0.01%. When you do, I would ask that you also reach down to help educate others so they too can join you.

Now, before we save the world, let's get back into some financial education.

It's important to know exactly what a municipal bond is. Let's start with defining a bond:

A bond is simply a piece of paper. On that paper it says: the amount borrowed, the amount of interest that must paid each year, and how long until the principal must be paid back in full. Companies like Microsoft and Apple can raise money by issuing bonds.

The government can also issue bonds, and so can municipalities, called "municipal bonds," or "muni bonds" for short.

It is important to know how muni bonds can fit into your wealth accumulation strategy. When you rise into higher tax brackets, you will want to reduce in every way possible the taxes on even your short to mid-term investments.

When a municipality wants to raise money, perhaps to build a bridge, they issue a bond—meaning that they borrow money from investors to build that bridge. The investors, called the "bondholders," get an interest payment for lending their money to the municipality. Many times, if they charge a toll to cross the bridge, that toll is used to pay the bondholders.

What is important to understand is that the interest payments from muni bonds are taxed very little, and, in some cases are completely tax-free. All muni bonds are free from federal income taxes, avoiding a tax as high as 39.6%. If you live in California (for example) and invest in California muni bonds, then California doesn't charge you state income taxes, a tax as high as 13.3%. Do the math and you can avoid a tax as high as 53% when investing in muni bonds, as long as you invest in the state that you live in.

Muni bonds have generally only been used by the wealthy, due to the historically high investment minimums before you can invest. Fortunately, today, the minimums to invest in muni bonds have come down with technology and the creation of ETF's, and even apps on your cell phone.

I personally invest into stocks, bonds, and muni bonds to save for short and mid-term goals such as "My Tesla Fund," or when socking away money for a vacation.

A muni bond won't make you wealthy, but it is much better than the .01% that the banks will pay you on your savings.

Personally, I don't have any money in my savings account. I have a checking account at a credit union, and investments accessed through Apps on my iPhone. There is a specific app that I use to invest for short and mid-term goals, but because I don't make specific recommendations in my books, you will have to do your own research to learn of the Apps available on your iPhone or Android.

You can invest with low minimums, while also getting access to muni bonds to avoid taxes. And, if invested in stocks for more than a year, you can lower your taxes with long-term capital gains taxes rather than paying income taxes.

In the next two chapters we will cover how the rich use "capital gains taxes" and "tax loss harvesting" to reduce their tax bill.

"You must pay taxes. But there's no law that says you have to leave a tip."
—Morgan Stanley Advertisement

CHAPTER FOUR

Tax-Avoidance Strategy #4:
Capital Gains Taxes

W ARREN BUFFETT, AT ONE TIME THE RICHEST MAN
in the world from investing, is quoted as saying,
"If you don't find a way to make money while you
sleep, you will work until the day you die."

Wealth accumulation is a game of inches: small wins over
the years, to slowly and consistently make money, avoid taxes,
and build residual income. "Residual income" is when you
have some sort of income or investment that earns money
with very little effort or work. It is "making money while
you sleep."

Your goal should be to build as many income streams as
possible, until your residual income exceeds your expenses.
When this happens, you are, by definition, financially
independent.

What is important to understand is that getting rid of payments has the same effect as creating another income stream.
For that reason, I avoid payments like they are a virus—while
simultaneously figuring out how to add more income streams
to my household.

Let me ask you:

Right now, how many income streams do you have?

For most, their answer is "one." They have a job, and must get up every day and go to work to earn a paycheck. And with changes in technology, millions of those jobs will disappear.

So what will you do if your job disappears, and with it, your only source of income?

Without financial literacy, I call a J.O.B. a **J**ail **O**perating as a **B**usiness.

Jokes aside:

A J.O.B. + Debt = Financial slavery to pay the banks and government.

The rich have one focus when it comes to their money: They run a business to make money, and they reinvest that money to generate even more money—which they funnel back into investments. They repeat the process until they become wealthy. I recommend that you do the same.

The rich also employ multiple tax avoidance strategies at one time when investing.

One strategy that can be used to reduce taxes is paying long-term capital gains taxes rather than income taxes.

A capital gain is the rise in value of an asset such as real estate or stocks.

You can have *short-term* or *long-term* capital gains.

> » *Short-term* is if you sold the asset prior to one year, and is taxed at the highest rates.
> » *Long-term* is if you held the asset more than one year, and is taxed at a lower rate.

I'm not sure where long-term capital gains tax rates will

be when you read this book, but they have historically been much less than income tax rates.

I remember the exact moment when I decided I wanted to become an investor. I learned that employees pay the highest tax rates, but investors can put their money to work for them and it will be taxed very little, or not taxed at all. I immediately liked my job less, and decided to learn everything I could about investing.

The solution is clear: You must make money work hard for you, so that one day you don't need to work for money.

The first and easiest way to put money to work for you is to start investing into mutual funds or ETF's. They are "diversified investments," meaning you are buying a basket of stocks as opposed to just buying one individual stock, which has more risk.

When you buy a mutual fund, or ETF, that can be one form of residual income, as the stocks and bonds pay dividend income. Today, in addition to stocks and bonds, muni bonds can be built inside of an ETF, and generate non-taxable dividend income.

If the stocks and bonds are held for more than one year, they are taxed at long-term capital gains tax rates rather than income tax rates. Combining these strategies results in double tax-avoidance!

The same is true for real estate, and almost all other types of investments: If held for more than one year, the taxes can be reduced by paying long-term capital gains taxes rather than income taxes.

I personally invest in stocks and ETFs when saving for short to mid-term goals. It far exceeds the 1%, or less, that they pay in savings accounts. And yes, the 1% that you earn at the banks is also taxable at the highest rates.

ETFs or mutual funds likely won't make you wealthy. But they are a good start to building residual income, and do not require much time or effort to invest.

Would it surprise you that the rich have a strategy to avoid taxes even when they lose money?

In the next chapter we will show you why "losing money" can be good news when it comes to taxes.

"The difference between death and taxes is that death doesn't get worse every time Congress meets."
—Will Rogers, Actor, Humorist & Newspaper Columnist

CHAPTER FIVE

Tax-Avoidance Strategy #5:
Tax-Loss Harvesting

THE RICH GENERALLY DON'T CARE IF THE MARKET
goes up, or if it goes down. They understand that there
is always an opportunity to make money.

If the market goes up, they can sell and take profit. If the
market goes down, they will simply buy more stock—when
those stocks are considered "undervalued," or "cheap."

As your income rises, so will your taxes, and the more
tax-avoidance strategies you will want to employ. The rich
use tax-loss harvesting in a market downturn to reduce their
taxes. And historically, this strategy has only been available
to the wealthiest of all Americans.

This strategy is to "harvest" any losses, which is done by:

» First selling a stock or ETF that has experienced
  a loss, then
» Immediately replacing it with another similar
  stock or ETF

This effectively creates a loss on their taxes. This "loss" can
offset both your past and future stock or ETF gains, and the

dividends received from them.

Tax-loss harvesting won't make you wealthy, but it can certainly be good news at tax time. It is also a strategy that I use in my own investing.

As I mentioned before, tax-loss harvesting was only available to the wealthy. But due to advances in technology, and computer algorithms, it is becoming more available to anyone—even those with a small amount of money to invest.

You will have to do your own research to find an advisor that is aware of the advantages of tax-loss harvesting, and can help you with this strategy.

Here is some food for thought:

In your future investing, if you hold your stock investments for more than a year, use tax-loss harvesting to reduce your taxes, and invest into muni bonds… is that triple tax avoidance?

Why yes, it is!

Now, let's cover the "Roth IRA" used by the rich.

If you would like more information on how Roth IRAs, capital gains taxes, municipal bonds, and tax-loss harvesting can reduce your taxes, text "Invest" to: (833) 455-4540 or Email: 10ways@REMiiGroup.com

PART THREE

LIFE INSURANCE FOR TAX AVOIDANCE

"Rule No. 1: Never lose money.
  Rule No. 2: Never forget rule No. 1."
—Warren Buffet

CHAPTER SIX

Tax-Avoidance Strategy #6:
The "Rich Man's Roth"

I T HELPS TO STUDY HISTORY AND UNDERSTAND HOW and when tax codes came about—especially when those strategies can help you avoid huge amounts of taxes. What is also important to know is that anyone with a "higher income" can't invest into Roth IRA's.

You should be asking the question, "If the rich can't use Roth IRA's, where do they put their money?"

Your next question should be, "And where do the banks put their money?"

If you guessed that the banks don't save their money in the bank—you are correct.

As you may recall in our story of the Four Brothers, Danny clearly got the best advice. After 40 years of investing, he had over $2,675,000 in his Roth IRA, completely exempt from all taxes.

The problem I hear all the time is, "I don't have 40 years to invest, so what do I do?"

Am I right to assume that you also don't have 40 years to invest?

As mentioned earlier, I don't have any money in a Roth IRA—partly because, I'm happy to say, I make too much money to fund a Roth IRA.

But there is one more important reason:

In my opinion, a Roth IRA is a poor choice for investing for those who want to build serious wealth—as millions of dollars is not worth "millions of dollars" 40 years from now.

The rich have a good understanding of Internal Revenue Code (IRC) Section 7702A, and the types of investments that can be sheltered under this tax code.

Tax code 7702 and 7702A, enacted in 1985, regulate how much money can be sheltered inside a life insurance policy. Yes, I know that may sound strange, but the rich, and the banks, shelter their investments inside life insurance policies to eliminate the taxes. In fact, they have billions of dollars sheltered inside this strategy.

Here are some basics about tax code 7702A:

» Similar to a Roth IRA, insurance policies must be funded with after-tax money.
» Under this tax code, gains earned inside a life insurance policy can be free of capital gains taxes, and eliminate the taxes on the dividends from both stocks and bonds.
» The gains can be accessed tax-free at any age.
» The money can be withdrawn for any reason: to go on a vacation, put a down payment on a house, fund your kid's college, or provide a supplemental tax-free income at retirement.
» Similar to a Roth IRA, distributions from an insurance policy are tax-free, and distributions

don't trigger taxation of your social security benefits.

» The money inside your policy, plus the death benefit, can be passed to your heirs tax-free.

» Unlike a regular Roth IRA, the "Rich Man's Roth" avoids probate.

When I first heard of this strategy, I was sold!

"No taxes?" I asked.

"That is correct. No taxes for the rest of your life. And no taxes when you die."

In 2005 I purchased my first policy, called a Variable Universal Life, or "VUL." I didn't have any life insurance at the time and I learned that I could get both permanent life insurance and tax benefits all in one policy. I began funding $250 a month to start.

Let's define VUL:

"Variable" means the value fluctuates with the value of the stock and bonds, called "subaccounts" within a VUL.

"Universal"—means it is very flexible as to how, and when I wanted to fund it. And finally, it is

"Life insurance" which is regulated by the IRS under tax code 7702A.

Today, I still own that VUL. And I am waiting for the next great stock market crash, so I can buy stocks afterwards, invest at the bottom (as close as possible), and grow my investments sheltered away from any taxes.

This is great, but the only downside of VULs is that I can still lose money, just like other investments in the market.

It was 2006 when a friend, Mike, who works in the insurance industry asked me a question:

"Mark, how would you like to invest without taxes, but also without any risk?"

He had my full attention.

"Tell me more Mike."

"Well, I noticed you have a new iPhone. Is it the latest model?"

"Yes it is. My last one broke so I just got a new one. The features are amazing! The camera is better and it has more storage, and it's thinner, faster, and lighter than my old phone. The commercial called it the 'Next Generation of iPhone.'"

"Well, just like cell phones, I want to show you 'the next generation' of life insurance policies. They are called 'IULs,' and they can't lose money."

Now, I was really intrigued.

"Come on Mike, how do they not lose money?"

"Well, although the money inside an IUL grows *based on the performance of* the stock market, the money inside an IUL is not actually invested in the market. Let me tell you the history of how IULs came about.

"First, have you ever heard the term 'Market-Linked CD'?"

"Nope," I replied.

"Well, the 'not losing money' part is not a new concept—it has been around a long time. At many of the biggest banks, you can buy investments that grow with the market, but they can't lose money. They call them 'Market-Linked CDs.

"Now, before you get too excited, let me give you the drawbacks of this investment.

"One, you will likely need a large lump sum of money to open one.

"And two, your gains would be taxable, similar to a CD."

"Well okay, but I don't have a large lump sum to invest, and I don't like the taxable part."

"Exactly Mark."

I was a little confused, "What do you mean?"

"Well, the insurance companies realized they could build a Market-Linked CD inside of a life insurance policy. Once sheltered under tax code 7702A, they could eliminate the taxes, and they could reduce the minimums so that anyone can invest. That is the 'next generation' of insurance policies."

"That sounds almost too good to be true."

"Well, for full disclosure, an IUL cannot lose money... but there is generally an annual 'cap,' meaning a maximum you can earn each year. It is around 13 percent, but depending on the IUL, it could be higher or lower."

I was astonished.

"So let me get this straight Mike. My investments make money like they are invested in the market, but I can't lose money? And I can earn up to 13 percent return per year? Plus, all my gains are tax-free because it is inside a life insurance policy?"

"Sounds like you got it. And what is similar to your VUL is there is a maximum amount of money you can contribute each year to the policy, based on the size of your death benefit. The bigger the policy, the more you can invest each year."

"How come I've never heard of an IUL before?" I asked.

"Well, like any of the best investments, it is always the wealthy that get them first. Then they eventually filter down to everyone else."

It was 2006 when I purchased my first IUL.

Let's first define IUL:

"Index," means the earnings are based on the performance of an index, such as the S&P 500.

"Universal," means that it is also very **flexible** as to how and when you fund it. And, finally

"Life insurance," means it comes with all the same tax benefits under tax code 7702A.

What is most interesting today about IULs is there have been many upgrades over the past 20 years. And the "next generation of IULs" have been released many times. Just like cell phone companies, insurance companies have been forced to upgrade their models each year to stay competitive.

Today, an IUL can provide:

» Inexpensive long-term care benefits as an add-on, also known as a "rider."

» Additional investment options have become available, such as international indexes, the Russell 2000, NASDAQ 100, the Dow Jones Industrial Average, and countless others—depending on the design of the IUL

» Unlike a Roth IRA, with a maximum contribution of $5500 a year, there is no limit to the amount you can contribute annually to an IUL. "The bigger the policy, the more you can invest each year."

» And, it has "rollover minutes." Unlike a Roth IRA, any year that you do not contribute the maximum each year to your IUL, that amount you didn't use "rolls over" to the next year. For example, if your maximum annual investment is $20,000 a year, and you only contributed $10,000 the first year, that next year you could contribute up to $30,000 without violating IRS tax code 7702A.

» Historically, IULs have had a "floor," where you can't lose your money— and a "cap," which is the maximum you could earn each year. But today, you may even find "uncapped" strategies—so you can invest with no risk, and no cap.

» And finally, available inside a handful of policies,
  you can have the option of investing with "Other
  People's Money (we will cover "OPM" in the next
  chapter). This option is sometimes called "alternate
  loans" and becomes invaluable after a stock market
  crash—where you didn't lose any money—and
  you can then borrow from the insurance company.
  This loan is secured by the cash value of your policy,
  giving you the opportunity to invest into stocks
  and real estate, without removing the cash value
  from your policy.

I'm going to let you in on a little secret. Fortune 500
executives, and the bankers themselves, have billions of
dollars inside of this type of strategy for one purpose only:
tax avoidance!

Now, if you are one of the Top 1%, I have exciting news
for you.

How about no taxes at all?

To read what is possible with IULs, you should Google an
article in Forbes magazine called, "How to Use Life Insurance
in Your Retirement Planning."

In this article, University of Michigan's Football Coach,
Jim Harbaugh, will retire at age 66 with 1.4 million dollars
a year from his IUL, all tax-free. What is most interesting
about this article is that Jim "earned" the money by taking
loans from the University rather than receiving a salary. Loans
are not taxable to Jim, whereas a salary would be highly taxed.

Once sheltered in his IUL, the money will grow tax-free
without chance of loss, his income will be tax-free, and at

his death, Jim will pass a large inheritance to his heirs… all completely tax-free.

"So, when did Jim pay taxes?" you ask.

The answer is, he never did. Jim never paid any taxes.

Oh, and it gets better for Jim. His IUL "income" he will receive at retirement will not cause his social security payments to be taxed. Jim will receive his 1.4 million a year tax-free, plus his social security payments will also be exempt from taxes.

As I stated before, "Tax avoidance becomes easier as your wealth increases."

You may be asking, "What about the loans Jim took from the University of Michigan? When does he have to pay them back?"

Yes, Jim will need to pay back the loans, just not from his own money, as the life insurance policy death benefit is large enough to pay back all the loans, plus any interest. And Jim will have a sizable tax-free death benefit left over to go to his heirs.

Now, I understand that you may not be able to do exactly what Jim Harbaugh did, but once you make your millions, you should find an advisor that specializes in "Premium Financing"—where your policy (just like Jim's) can be funded with "loans," which are not taxable, and use "Other People's Money" to fund your tax-advantaged IUL.

Turn to the next chapter to learn of the power of using "OPM."

If you would like more information on the "Rich Man's Roth," text "IUL" to: (833) 455-4540
or Email: 10ways@REMiiGroup.com

PART FOUR

REAL ESTATE & "OPM"

"For a Nation to try and tax itself into prosperity is like a man standing in a bucket trying to lift himself up by the handle."

—Winston Churchill,
Prime Minster of the United Kingdom

CHAPTER SEVEN

Tax-Avoidance Strategy #7:
Buy a Home using "OPM"

I T IS UNFORTUNATE, BUT OF THOSE IN AMERICA THAT can "retire comfortably," many only do so because they make one very important investment in their lives: they buy a home.

And without their home (hopefully it is paid off) and social security income, many would work until the day that they die.

What is more unfortunate, is that the middle class employs the same strategy used by the wealthiest of all Americans—to make exponentially high rates of returns on their money, without fully understanding why the strategy works so well.

They are using "leverage," or OPM to invest.

Using OPM is one of the key strategies to building significant wealth.

The most common example of using OPM is borrowing from a bank to buy real estate.

Let's first make a comparison of using OPM when buying real estate, vs using only your own money.

Let me introduce you to Mr. Conservative, and Mr. Risky. Both Mr. Conservative and Mr. Risky inherited $300,000.

Mr. Conservative, after receiving his inheritance, asked his dad, "What should I do with the money?"

"Do the smart thing and buy a home. Pay cash so you don't have a mortgage payment."

Mr. Conservative followed his dad's advice, and purchased a $300,000 home with cash. He was proud to own it without having a mortgage payment.

» Assuming his home was appreciating by 5% each year, or $15,000, after 10 years his home was worth $450,000.

» After 30 years, Mr. Conservative felt accomplished. He was able to go into retirement, partially because he had no mortgage. He had arrived safely, and his home was worth $750,000.

» Unfortunately, at age 67, Mr. Conservative realized he had invested very little for retirement, and his social security would not provide enough income to live the lifestyle that he desired. So, to supplement his income, he was forced to refinance his home into a "reverse mortgage," more recently known as a Home Equity Conversion Mortgage, or "HECM."

His HECM mortgage provided him the extra income he needed for retirement. However, he passed less money to his heirs as the HECM loan was eating away at his equity.

So, did Mr. Conservative make the right decision when paying cash for his home?

Let's read on to see how Mr. Risky did.

———

Mr. Risky, after receiving his inheritance from his rich uncle—we will call him "Uncle Mark"—also asked, "What should I do with the money?"

With a smile, Uncle Mark responded, "Do the smart thing and buy ten homes. Rent them all so the tenants pay down the mortgages for you.

"Only put 10 percent down, or $30,000 to buy each property, and have the bank put up the other 90 percent of the money. That is an example of using 'Other People's Money,' or 'OPM.' Your properties will be purchased with 90 percent of the banks money rather than using your own."

"I've never heard of 'OPM' before," said Mr. Risky. "What is that?"

"Well, OPM is when you use a small amount of your own money to control, and own, a much larger asset. In this case, you will own $3,000,000 worth of real estate, but you will only have put up $300,000 of your own money. The bank put up the other $2,700,000. And, you get to keep all the appreciation of the real estate. Sounds pretty good doesn't it?

"Yes, that does sound good."

"But do you want to know the best part about using OPM to invest?" Uncle Mark asked.

"What's that?"

"Well this will require a little math, but let me illustrate the numbers:

» "You will have invested $300,000 of your own money to own $3,000,000 worth of real estate.

» "If your real estate appreciates 5% per year, or $150,000 each year, it will increase in value by $1,500,000 in ten years.

» "That's a total value of $4,500,000 – a 500% rate of return on your money.

» "After 30 years, your properties will have increased in value to $7,500,000. You will have turned your $300,000 inheritance into 7.5 million dollars!"

That is the power and multiplying effect of using OPM to invest.

Now, having seen this, which investor would you rather be? Mr. Conservative? Or Mr. Risky?

Yes, the above examples are over-simplified and don't account for the fees and commissions paid when buying or selling real estate, or the fact that Mr. Risky would have to rent the properties over thirty years. The point I'm trying to make is that rich people use OPM to earn a much higher rate of return on their money.

Again, if you want to build great wealth, you too will have to use OPM.

Now, since this is a book on tax avoidance, let's spend a bit of time on how home ownership helps you reduce taxes.

For those who have never owned a home, the tax deductions—aka tax avoidance—are based on the amount of *interest* you pay on your mortgage each month.

For example: The mortgage payment on a $300,000 home is about $1610 a month when using a 5% interest rate. $1250 of the $1610 goes to pay the interest (initially) leaving only $360 to pay down the principal. The total amount to interest for that year would be $15,000.

That would be a tax deduction of $15,000 by owning rather than renting.

Here is the question you should ask:

"How many places can I safely get a high rate of return on my money, year after year, and get tax deductions at the same time?"

The answer is, you must use the same strategies as the wealthy. And they love to use OPM.

Later in the book, we will get into more examples of ways to achieve a much higher rate of return using OPM.

In addition, we will cover how to use OPM, and then use OPM again to earn an even higher rate of return. And yes, we will show you how to do it with a high degree of safety.

In the next chapter, we will cover how your primary residence can earn you up to $500,000, completely free of federal income taxes, state income taxes, and capital gains taxes.

Yes, up to $500,000, completely tax-free!

"You don't pay taxes—they take taxes."
—Comedian Chris Rock

CHAPTER EIGHT

Tax-Avoidance Strategy #8:
$250,000/$500,000
Home Sale Exemption

A S I WROTE ABOUT IN *RICH MAN POOR BANK*, I FELT scammed after attending business school back in Canada. After learning nothing about how money works, I soon dropped out of school and moved to California. After arriving in Los Angeles, I began calculating all of my student loans and credit card debts.

I began to ask myself, *How is it that the only thing that I took away from college was student loans and credit card debts?*

How did that happen?

Within a few years, I had established a stable income and was even able to buy a condominium in Van Nuys, CA. I had begun to read books and study how money works. I learned first-hand how to use OPM to buy my condo, putting only 3.5% as a down payment, or about $5000, and borrowing the rest from the bank.

When making my mortgage payment, the interest deduction offset my income, and reduced my taxes that I owed each year.

Fortunately for me, I had also bought my condo at a great time when home prices began to appreciate very rapidly in California. My property, which I had purchased two years earlier for $140,000, was now valued at $260,000. I had earned $120,000!

I was excited to pay off all my student loans and credit card debts, and I decided to sell my condo. That is when the tax avoidance "magic" happened.

My conversation with my tax advisor went something like this:

"Good day Mr. Quann, I've got all your receipts and W2's to finish your taxes, but I just have one more question. How long did you live in the condominium that you sold?"

"A little over two years."

He smiled. "Okay great. Then you won't have to pay any taxes on the sale."

"Really?"

"Yes Mark. In fact, you could have earned up to $250,000 and not had to pay taxes on any of it—providing that you lived there for at least two of the past five years."

"Two of the last five years? What does that mean?"

"Well, you could have lived in it for two years, then rented it for three years, and upon the sale you would qualify for the exemption. Or rented it for three years, then lived in it for two years, and still qualify for the exemption. As long as you lived there at least 'two of the past five years.'

"The gains, up to $250,000 would be completely tax-free. Married couples have double the exemption, and can earn up to $500,000 which would be exempt from taxes."

I ran the numbers in my head and calculated how long it would take me to save my after-tax income and accumulate $120,000. It could take decades.

I then took out my iPhone and quickly calculated the return on my initial investment. I had paid out of pocket $5,000 to buy my condominium, and walked away with $120,000 tax-free in two years. I had earned 2400% return on my money, and avoided paying a penny in taxes on all the gains. Wow!

My next question to my tax advisor was an obvious one. "Can I do it again?"

"Yes Mark, you can."

It was not long before I bought another property, lived in it for two years, and upon the sale, I used the home sale exemption.

Several years later, after the crash of 2007-2008, when I figured that real estate prices had hit rock bottom, I bought another home for $360,000. Exactly 2 years later I sold it for $515,000, and again, I used the same exemption.

To most people, buying real estate is an emotional decision, as they think of it as their "home." Traditionally, they would live in it their entire life and dream of the day they send that last mortgage payment in the mail. They throw a party and invite all their friends to celebrate actually "owning" their home.

I think that this a great plan... if you only plan to be middle class.

There are many advisors that will tell you to do the same. In fact, it is more common than not.

But this book is not "How to Retire Comfortably in the Middle Class." If it were, I'd be suggesting the following:

» Contribute to your IRA to save money on taxes
» Maximize the contributions to your 401(k)
» Here is how to get an 800 credit score

» Be sure to keep at least $50,000 in your savings
account for emergencies.
» Lastly, buy a house and pay it off quickly so you
can live your Golden Years without a mortgage
payment.

This book is for those that want to accumulate wealth.
And, to accumulate wealth in real estate, I decide the *purpose* of real estate before I buy it. I ask myself the following
questions:

**Am I buying it to live in it for a minimum of two years,
with the plan of selling it for tax-free gains?**

**Will I rent it for a few years, then live in it for two years—
so that I can convert what would be taxable gains to
tax-free income?**

Perhaps one day I'll buy a house and live in it for the rest
of my life, but I doubt it. Taking profits of up to $250,000
tax free is just too tempting—especially when I know how to
take the tax-free gains and shelter them into my IUL (aka my
"Rich Man's Roth") and then grow it with no risk, and no taxes.
As of today, in 2018, here is a summary of where we stand
as a country:

» Almost a decade ago, the federal reserve printed
trillions of dollars to try and save the economy.
» Just as I wrote about in *Rich Man Poor Bank,* that
money is now "chasing the same amount of goods
and services, causing prices to rise,"— inflation.
» Real Estate and stock prices have been soaring,
and I expect they will continue to do so for an
unforeseen amount of time.

But, as the saying goes, "Whatever goes up must come down."

Perhaps, like me, you are thinking, "When is the next crash coming, and how big will it be?"

The answer is, no one *really* knows.

But with money skills, you should construct a plan to make money when stocks and real estate go up, and have a plan to make more money after they crash—buying more stocks and real estate when prices are low.

Have you heard the expression "buy low, sell high"?

Be sure to also have a plan for tax avoidance the next time you buy real estate. If done properly, with the guidance of a CPA or other tax professional, you can pay my favorite type of taxes: No taxes at all!

Lastly, while building wealth, it helps to understand that the economy only does two things:

It expands—causing prices to rise.

Or it contracts—causing prices to fall.

The best investors have a plan for both.

When picking your advisors, they should know how to make money in either case, and be familiar with all ten of the tax avoidance strategies.

The bad news is another crash is coming. We just don't know when, or what will cause it.

But if you are one of the few that has lots of cash on hand, and money in IULs, a crash can be a great time to build wealth, especially when investing using OPM. Remember, it is not "if," but "when" the market will crash next.

Now, before we close out this chapter, I think it is about time I let you know how to use OPM, and use it again, for even more leverage to invest… and do it with safety to earn even higher rates of returns on your money.

Are you ready?

The strategy is simple:

It involves using what are sometimes called "alternate loans" when borrowing from an IUL.

Covered briefly in Chapter 6, this type of loan is available in a handful of IULs, and gives you the ability to borrow money at a low interest rate, secured by the cash value in your policy. This leaves all your money inside the IUL to continue to grow safely.

It is important to remember that IULs can't lose money— even in a market crash—and the money can be accessed as a "loan" without paying taxes. And it can be done at any age.

So, after a market crash, you can use an "alternate loan" to borrow against the money in your IUL to buy real estate. If you put 10% down as a payment to buy property, you would be using the insurance companies' money (first OPM) and then using the banks money (OPM again) to purchase the real estate.

And yes, in the above case, you can do it with a high degree of safety—if buying the right piece of real estate after the crash.

To summarize: The rich make money when the economy grows, and make more money after an economic collapse. The great news is… you can do it too!

"Be sure you pay your taxes; otherwise you will get in a lot of trouble."
—Richard "Tricky Dick" Nixon
37th President of the United States

CHAPTER NINE

Tax-Avoidance Strategy #9:
Depreciation on Rental Property

I N CHAPTER FOUR YOU LEARNED HOW "HARVESTING"
the losses from your stock or ETF portfolio can help
you avoid taxes. Now we will cover why you want your
real estate to go down in value. That is correct, I said, "Why
you want your real estate to go down in value." Well, sort of.

Depreciation is an accounting term used to measure how
much the things you buy in your business will go down in
value each year.

For example: If you buy a chair for your business, your
tax advisor will tell you how much you can deduct from
your taxes each year as that chair loses its value. Per the IRS,
a chair will lose all its value after 7 years.

What is important to know is that it doesn't matter if what
you bought is actually going up or down in value. You get to
take the tax deduction regardless. Now, if you buy a chair, it
will very likely go down in value.

But what happens when you buy rental property?

Just like the chair, your rental property is a part of your
business. Your tax advisor will calculate how much your

property will "go down in value" each year—which can offset rents received from tenants living in the property. You get the tax deduction each year, even if your property goes up in value. This is sometimes called a "phantom expense or 'paper loss,'" and only applies to real estate when rented.

Yes, as a normal circumstance, your real estate will go up in value. But you get to say it is going down in value—to save you taxes!

Pretty cool, right?

In the simple example below, we will show you why owning rental property is so effective for tax avoidance.

⁓

Upon buying my first rental property many years ago, my CPA explained, "Well Mark, you can't depreciate the land under your rental property. You can only depreciate the value of the property itself—excluding the land. So we have to calculate two things:

"How much is the land worth?

"And, how much is the property worth?

"After running the numbers, your property itself is worth $336,000. Rental properties are depreciated over 27.5 years. So we take $336,000 and divide it by 27.5 years. That is $12,218 per year.

"Per the IRS, and according to accounting principles, your rental property will go down in value by $12,218 each year. And you get to deduct that amount from your income. That is about $1,018 each month."

"Really?"

"Yes, but just to clarify, you only get to deduct that amount from your taxes providing you are collecting rental income from the tenants living in the property. So if you collected rent of $1,018, and had depreciation of $1,018, you would pay no taxes on that rental income. Does that make sense?"

"Yes, it does! It sounds like I get to collect rent, increase my income and not pay taxes on that income, *legally*."

"And that is why they call it a 'phantom loss.'"

"It sounds like legal tax avoidance to me."

My CPA then added, "It is important to understand, you can't generally 'double dip' when it comes to tax codes. Let me explain.

"If you buy a property, you must decide first if you plan to rent it long term and use the depreciation deduction to reduce your taxes, or if you plan to sell it after two years and use the 'home sale exemption' to eliminate the taxes on your gains. You can't do both.

"Let's say for example you started renting a property and took the depreciation over several years, but then you decided to sell the property. You would get a tax bill upon the sale because the IRS would *recapture* all the years you took that depreciation—regardless if you lived in it for two years. They call this 'depreciation recapture.' And whatever phantom losses you took, you would be required to pay income taxes on them."

"So, what you are saying is that when I'm buying a property, I need to decide what the specific *purpose* is before I buy it—either as a rental, or to live in?"

"Well, sort of. You can do both. But if you plan to sell the property, you wouldn't want to take the depreciation, as you would lose all the benefits as soon as you sold the property.

"Lastly, be aware of advisors out there giving bad advice. Just yesterday, I had another client come into my office asking me for guidance. He had an advisor telling him to put his real estate into an IRA 'to avoid the taxes.' I told him to stay far away from that advisor, as once you put real estate into an IRA, you lose all the other deductions—including the interest deduction, the deduction from paying property taxes, the personal home sale exemption, and the depreciation.

"As a general rule, I don't recommend mixing retirement accounts and real estate. Real estate in itself has huge tax advantages already. All the advantages will disappear if you mix the two."

Okay, thus far we have covered

- » How to avoid taxes when you earn your money
- » How to avoid taxes when you spend your money
- » How to avoid taxes when you invest
- » How to avoid taxes when you sell your investments
- » And how to retire tax-free

But what about when you die?

Let's jump in to the next chapter and discover a powerful tax avoidance strategy: Die!

PART FIVE

MORE TAX AVOIDANCE

"I'd like somebody to get rid of the death tax. That's what I want. I don't want to get taxed just because I died. I just don't think it's right. If I give something to my kid, I already paid the tax.

"Why should I have to pay it again because I died?"

—Whoopi Goldberg, Actor

CHAPTER TEN

Tax-Avoidance Strategy #10:
"Die!"

I T MAY SOUND CRAZY, BUT SITTING IN THAT HOSPITAL bed—with needles in both arms and oxygen to help me breathe—I began thinking, *At least I'm worth a lot of money if I die.*

I even logged into my accounts, double checked that my beneficiaries were correct, and I verified how much life insurance I had. I made sure I had an updated Will and Trust, and I signed a Power of Attorney which would give the power to my sister to make my future health decisions, in the case I was not able to myself.

The reason I was so concerned is because of what Dr. Cunningham had told me:

"Mark, we are going to have to stop your heart and hook you up to a bypass machine to pump your blood and run your lungs, which can cause 'a long list of bad things.'"

Today, at least I have a pretty cool story to tell at parties.

"Want to hear how my heart stopped beating for 142 minutes?"

Yes, some people will say that talking about death, and how you are taxed, "sounds crazy."

But the fact is, death is coming for us all. We don't know how or when it will arrive. But when it comes, if you don't have a plan for your money, *someone else* does. That "someone" is Uncle Sam. His plan involves taxes, and lots of them.

So you have a choice to make:

You can go through life, ignoring death, and do very little planning. And when you die, your family may be left in bad shape financially. If you have any assets left, after taxation eats away a large chunk, your heirs will likely mismanage them, paying even more taxes. And soon, all your hard work will be gone.

Or,

You can live a very long life, and have a plan to avoid taxes. One day you'll pass a large amount of money to your heirs, yes, tax-free. And once received by your heirs, they can reinvest in tax-exempt investments and safely multiply your family's net worth many times over. And your grandkids can do the same.

Which plan sounds good to you?

I'm assuming you chose option two. And I should cover how dying can be such an effective tax avoidance strategy.

Let's quickly summarize the basics:

Life Insurance: The proceeds from life insurance, plus any investments built inside a life insurance policy, are exempt from all types of taxes. This is just another reason why the rich are so attracted to having investments sheltered inside a life insurance policy.

Stocks: When a person dies, the gains inherited in a stock account get what is called a "step-up in basis." This means the beneficiaries will receive the stock completely tax-free.

Real Estate: Real estate also can have a "step-up in basis" to eliminate the taxes, but you will need to review your exact situation with your tax professional.

So, are you ready to use all Top Ten Ways to Avoid Taxes?

How about a bonus Tax Avoidance Strategy?

"The tax code is a monstrosity and there's only one thing to do with it. Scrap it, kill it, drive a stake through its heart, bury it and hope it never rises again to terrorize the American people."
—Steve Forbes, Forbes Magazine

CHAPTER ELEVEN

Tax-Avoidance Strategy #11:
"Don't Live in California"

I F YOU WANT TO AVOID TAXES, YOU CAN'T LIVE IN OR have a business in California… or Connecticut, or Hawaii, or Illinois, or Iowa, or Maine, or Minnesota, or Maryland, or Mississippi, or New Jersey, or New York, or Ohio, or Rhode Island, or Vermont, or West Virginia. These states are the top 15 most highly taxed.

In California, over 52% of your paycheck can be taken when you add up state and federal income taxes, and a few other miscellaneous taxes.

I have a dilemma: Do I choose "perfect weather and sunshine all year long"? Or, do I chose "less taxes"?

The answer is really, "both."

I choose to reduce taxes as much as possible by owning a business and a corporation, and invest my after-tax income in the "Top Ten Ways to Avoid Taxes," which as you learned can eliminate any further taxation.

But here is the bad news:

When your income rises into the multiple six figures, even after all your tax deductions, you may find yourself stuck in the 40-52% tax rate on the highest portion of your income, regardless of which state you live in.

Would you like to know the good news?

The good news is that if you decide to move to a different state, we are going to cover how to avoid more taxes, and even buy tax-free supercars and real estate with your potential tax savings.

The strategy is simple: Move your business and your residence outside of one of the most highly taxed states.

And, purchase your supercar using a corporation registered in another lower-taxed state.

I learned of this strategy while sitting in a hot tub with my friend Justin. He had just moved his business from California to Austin, Texas. I arrived at the house a little before sunset, and I could not help but notice the stunning red Ferrari in the driveway. Next to the Ferrari was a silver Porsche convertible, bearing Montana license plates. As I entered the house I remember thinking, *Montana? That's far away.*

I knew Justin had moved his business to save on taxes, but I was a little shocked to find the amount of taxes that Justin had actually saved.

Our conversation began as we cracked open an ice cold Corona, and entered his hot tub.

"So Justin, how are you enjoying living in Austin?"

"I like it. There are things I like about both states. I obviously miss the weather in California, especially in the summer when temperatures get pretty extreme here. But I find the people are more friendly and down to earth here. And as you know, I don't miss the high taxes in California."

"Oh yeah. That is one thing we have in common. I don't like the taxes either."

"Why don't you move?"

"I gotta say, being from Canada, I'm highly addicted to perfect weather. I love to ride a Harley on the Pacific Coast Highway, and I do the same thing when I'm on vacation in Hawaii. I just can't get myself to move. So I write those checks to the tax man each year."

"Mark, did I ever tell you how much money I actually saved from moving?"

I smiled, "No, you didn't, and I'm awfully curious."

"Well, as you know, I used to have both my main office and my shipping center in California. I first decided to move my inventory and my shipping center to Texas. It saved me a lot of money in state taxes and payroll taxes.

"I was happy, and so were my employees. They no longer had to pay the state taxes, and the housing prices are much lower here so I helped a few of my employees to buy a home. They own rather than rent, so they even pay less in taxes.

"It seemed my employees were getting all the benefits, until one day I sat with my tax accountant and began to crunch the numbers to see my potential tax saving if I decided to move."

"My jaw about fell to the floor. I remember saying, '*That is how much I can save?*'

"'That's the amount,' my CPA responded.

"I went home and began to pack up the house, and told the kids we were moving to Texas."

"How much did you save?" I was curious.

"Well, you see this house?"

"Yes."

"And you saw the Ferrari in the driveway?"

I smiled again as I sipped my Corona, "Couldn't miss that!"

"Well Mark, they were both free."

With a somewhat confused look, I asked, "What do you mean, *free?*"

"They were 'free.' I paid for both of them with my tax savings. When you add it up, the amount of state taxes that I was paying to run my business in California, and the amount I was paying in personal income taxes, pays my entire mortgage and Ferrari payment. And I still have money left over."

I laughed, "That seems almost unbelievable. What did you do with your house in California?"

"We rent it out. We found some great tenants. We get the appreciation of California real estate, and the deductions from having a rental property, and we avoid most of the taxes because of the depreciation. All we had to give up was the weather. I also saved a big chunk of cash when I bought the Ferrari. It was nice to avoid the state taxes there too." Justin smiled.

"I gotta say Justin, that is awfully temping... a free house, and a Ferrari just for moving out of California? I may have to give it some more thought."

"How is business with you Mark?"

"It's fantastic, thanks for asking. I'm always expanding, and I really love what I do. It was 13 years ago that I quit my job, and decided I will never work for another person again. I'm glad I did, as today I work when I want, I can make more money when I want, and as a reward for all my hard work I'm even on the waiting list for a new Tesla Model 3."

"Are you going to buy it in Montana?" Justin asked.

"Montana? Why would I do that? I don't want to move to Montana, that's for sure."

"No of course not. But I'm sure you saw the Porsche in the driveway?"

"Kind of hard to miss. I also noticed it had Montana plates, and *was* sort of curious about that."

"Well, that is my cousin's car. He doesn't live in Texas, and he doesn't live in Montana either, he actually lives in Mississippi. Only his car is registered in Montana."

"Why did he do that?"

"For one reason Mark, taxes.

"My cousin was telling me how he avoided paying Mississippi state taxes when he registered a corporation in Montana. He purchased his car through his Limited Liability Corporation (LLC) rather than as a resident of Mississippi. He then rents the car from his Montana corporation. He dodged the taxes and the high registration fees in Mississippi by doing that. Using this strategy will be even more effective for you, living in California, since the taxes there are even higher."

"How come I've never heard of this before?"

"This is just another way that the rich avoid taxes—using corporations, and a little creativity. You can do it too, but you should talk with your CPA and weigh out the potential risks and rewards of using this strategy. It is legal, but it doesn't mean California likes it."

"I will for sure, thanks for the tip. I may even have to put that in my next book."

And that is the story of how this chapter ended up in this book.

To summarize:

» You can save a lot in taxes by moving a portion of, or all of your business and/or your residence outside of the most highly taxed states.

» That savings could in fact buy you a house, and maybe even a tax-free supercar.

» If you live in a highly taxed state, you may want to consider buying your supercar using a corporation registered in Montana, then rent/lease the car from your corporation.

But please consult with a licensed, highly competent tax professional before considering any of the above.

Okay, I can't help it... I just can't end the book here.

I have a couple more bonus chapters for you. They are not having to do with tax avoidance. But since we are talking about avoiding taxes for the purpose of building wealth, I think they have an important place in this book.

PART SIX:

ADVANCED WEALTH-BUILDING STRATEGIES

(And an update on Jack & Ellen)

"If you get up early, work late, and pay your taxes, you will get ahead— if you strike oil."

—John Paul Getty, American-British Industrialist and at one time "One of the wealthiest people in the world"

CHAPTER TWELVE

Wealth Accumulation Strategy #1:
A "Principal First" Mortgage

"**G**OOD DAY JOHN (NOT HIS REAL NAME), NICE TO meet you. If you step into our board room, we can start our meeting in just a few minutes. Would you like some coffee or water?"

"No thanks," John replied.

Within a few minutes, John was sitting with a top banking executive. We will call him "Mr. Bankster." John and Mr. Bankster began their meeting to discuss a mortgage that "Pays Principal First."

After some brief small talk, they got right into it.

"So John, I've never heard of a 'Principal First Mortgage.' How does it work?"

"Well Mr. Bankster, this type of mortgage is used in other countries, and combines your checking account and your mortgage into one."

"Sounds interesting."

"The mortgage works like this: At night, all the lazy money in the client's checking account is swept onto the client's mortgage principal, therefore reducing the amount of interest paid by the homeowner."

Mr. Bankster looked a little confused, and a bit frustrated, "Well, how would our customers get access to cash, if *all* their money had been swept onto their mortgage principal?"

"Great question Mr. Bankster!

"Well, this mortgage is not a traditional mortgage, rather it is set up as a credit line. And as I mentioned, any money that remains in your checking account is swept onto your mortgage principal that night. The next day when you need money, you simply use your debit card, or write a check as you normally would do. And only that amount is swept back from your credit line, increasing your mortgage balance by that amount, which arrives in your checking account to clear the transaction."

"John, let me clarify what you are asking of us. You want us to apply all the savings of our customers directly to their mortgage principal every night, potentially cannibalizing billions of interest to the bank?"

"Yes, Mr. Bankster, that is *exactly* what I'm proposing."

Mr. Bankster, after choking on his coffee, thanked him for his time and promptly ended the meeting.

While exiting the room, he asked one last question, "We are not interested in offering this type of mortgage at our bank, but I may be interested in it for myself. Can you leave your business card and a brochure with my secretary?"

—

Yes, this actually happened at one of the mega-banks.

What you likely don't know is that there are *some* mortgages available in other parts of the world that are virtually unknown to most Americans—as the banking executives themselves would be fired for making such a proposal.

These mortgages, which are credit lines tied to a checking account, can save huge amounts of interest, and completely destroy the need to ever have a savings account again.

As with any financial product, these types of mortgages, *if used properly,* can save you huge amounts of money in interest versus a traditional thirty-year mortgage. It can also reduce the time it would take to pay off the mortgage to a fraction of the time.

Those that own rental properties can also use this strategy: You would leverage the rents received from your tenants, and use that income to supercharge payoff of your primary residence.

Once paid off, and looking to buy another rental property, you can simply write a check for the down payment—eliminating the need to get another mortgage.

And then simply repeat the process: The rents from that new property can be used to supercharge payoff the new amount borrowed from the credit line. You can do this too, repeating the process until you become a very wealthy real estate mogul.

If used properly, by a highly disciplined person that loves to save money, this type of mortgage can be a powerful tool.

Now, since we covered the good things about this mortgage, I also want to spend time on "the bad."

It would be a very bad idea for a "spender" to use this type of mortgage, as it can turn the equity of their home into an "ATM machine."

This type of loan has a "variable rate," which is recommended only to highly professional, highly financially educated, and highly disciplined investors.

This type of mortgage has had different names over the years, and the names may be different depending on which bank or credit union offers the loan. For that reason, I've decided to not put the name in this book. Be sure to talk with a licensed mortgage professional who is knowledgeable about the advantages and the disadvantages of this type of mortgage.

"The more you learn, the more you earn."
—Frank Clark, US Congressman

CHAPTER THIRTEEN

Wealth Accumulation Strategy #2:
A Reverse Mortgage to Help You Build Wealth

W HENEVER I MENTION THE WORDS, "REVERSE mortgage," the response is always the same: People immediately shut off any explanation I have, and after I'm gone, they call their friends and rant, "Mark Quann suggested a reverse mortgage when I turn 62. He wants me to lose my home when I die. I'll never let that guy into my home again!"

"Well, that didn't go as intended."

Let me make a statement that may sound controversial, and nothing like what you have ever heard before:

I suggest a reverse mortgage to everyone when they turn 62— especially those that want to build, protect, and accumulate wealth, and pass more money to their heirs.

Traditionally, a reverse mortgage is used by those that didn't save enough money for retirement and they need additional income. In order to get access to cash, they tap into the equity of their home—either as an income stream, or a lump sum payment—to pay for medical needs, or the other costs of retirement.

Yes, a reverse mortgage does the opposite of a regular mortgage: Your mortgage balance goes up rather than down, because the income you take, plus the interest on the loan, is added to your mortgage balance—effectively eating away at the equity of your home.

But the thing to remember is that most people that use a reverse mortgage do so because they *have to*. They don't have a choice. But, what about the people that *don't need* a reverse mortgage?

They do so because they simply *want one*?

"What?" you may be asking?

Here is what is important to understand: All mortgages—whether fixed for thirty years, or those that "pay principal first," or even reverse mortgages—can be both "good" and "bad."

The key is understanding how to *hedge* your position when using a reverse mortgage—to actually *create* more wealth.

The term "hedge" is used in investing. It basically means that when you do something, such as invest, you also do something that "bets in the other direction"—making you money regardless of the outcome of the investment.

For example: A life insurance policy pays your family if you *die too soon*. A long-term care policy protects your assets if you *live too long*. So by owning both life insurance and long-term care, you are covered if you "die too soon," or "live too long" and need help with your daily activities in your elderly years. That's "hedging."

To cover this strategy in detail, let me tell you about a meeting I had with Jack and Ellen.

Remember Jack and Ellen? The couple we first met in *Rich Man Poor Bank*?

I had arrived at Jack's accounting practice just before 9 AM, and he immediately called me in.

"Hi Jack, it has been quite a while. How have you been? And how are Ellen and the kids?" I asked.

"They are all great. Thanks for asking. It is amazing how fast they grow up, and how the time flies by.

"When are you going to have kids Mark? Be sure to not wait too long. You don't want to be old and grey and still raising them."

"All in good time Jack… all in good time. I do think about it more often when seeing my brother take his two kids to the hockey games. I see how much fun he has raising his boys."

"Mark, it seemed like it was just yesterday that Ellen and I first met you and we got all of our finances in order. In fact, I want to thank you again for your advice. If it was not for your guidance over the years, I know we would not be doing this well financially. And, don't tell Ellen that I told you this, but we don't argue about money anymore.

"We followed your advice, eliminated much of our debt, funded both our Roth IRA's and placed some money into mutual funds. We funded our IULs, and we refinanced from a thirty-year loan to a fifteen-year loan. Because of you Mark, we will own our home fifteen years earlier. When the day comes, with money in our 401(k)s, Social Security to supplement our income, mutual funds, Roth IRA's, and extra income from our IULs, we will be in great shape when we finally retire. All thanks to you."

Just then, Ellen popped her head in the door with, "Sorry I am a bit late, traffic was horrible."

Behind Ellen was a woman who appeared to be in her mid 60's, and a man of about the same age. They all came into the office.

Jack looked over at me, "Mark, these are my parents, Linda and Paul."

I smiled, "Great to meet you Linda. Great to meet you Paul."

I got out of my chair and they both shook my hand warmly. They seemed excited to meet me.

Jack looked over at me again, "Well Mark, the reason for our meeting today is not to meet with Ellen and I. It's actually because my parents want to retire soon, and I told them how creative you were with our finances. We talked it over, and they want to get your advice on what you would suggest for their retirement."

"I'd be happy to help. Anything specific you want me to look at?" I asked Paul.

"We just want you to look at everything we have. We don't want to run out of money in our retirement. We are both very healthy, so we could have a lot of years left. We want to vacation, and we love to spend time with our grandkids. Linda and I plan to work a few more years because we both still enjoy it. Right, Hun?"

"Yes, that is true."

Linda then handed me an envelope, "Here Mark, that is all of our finances. Jack told me exactly what we needed to bring to be prepared for the meeting."

I opened the envelope, "Can you give me a few minutes to look this over?"

"Sure, take all the time you need. We actually are planning a family vacation to Hawaii, and need to coordinate with Jack and Ellen. We'll go get some coffee while you look that over and be back in 15 minutes. Would you like anything?"

"No thanks." I replied.

The four of them left the office.

About 15 minutes later, Jack, Linda and Paul sat back down in the office.

"Will Ellen be joining us Jack?" I asked

"No, she went back home to check on the kids."

After some small talk, Linda asked, "So Mark, what did you learn about our finances?"

"Well, it looks like you guys are doing great. You don't have any credit card debt or auto loans, and you've saved a good chunk for retirement in your 401(k). Does that sound about right?"

"Yes, that sounds about right."

"I have some questions for you both. Is your goal to spend down your money and leave whatever is left over to your heirs? Or do you want to leave them a larger legacy?"

"I think we would like to do both. Right, Paul?"

"Yes, we would like to do both, *if* that is possible."

"I think it is. But we need to do some out-of-the-box thinking," I commented.

"Out of the box?" Linda asked.

"Yes, I have some ideas, but I have to ask that you keep an open mind, and hear me out before you come to a conclusion. Can we agree on that?"

"We are always open to learn. Let's hear this 'out-of-the-box thinking' so we can take more vacations with the grandkids." Linda smiled.

"Well, I am recommending two things:

"First, I suggest we evaluate the benefits of a long-term care policy for the both of you."

Paul jumped in, "I've considered long-term care policies before, but they are just too pricey. We would rather use that money for other things in retirement."

"Have you ever heard of *hybrid* policies?" I asked.

"No, what is a hybrid policy?"

"Well, I know you may have priced-out regular, standalone long-term care policies, and you are correct—they tend to be very expensive.

"But over the years, many insurance companies, in order to stay competitive, have created 'hybrid' life insurance policies that combine both life insurance and long-term care into one. The long-term care is actually a *'rider'* on the life insurance policy, which brings down the cost. They are *very* inexpensive when compared to regular long-term care policies. The life insurance provides a death benefit in the event that one of you die, and the long-term care is there for both of you, if you ever need it."

Linda looked over at me, "What is a 'rider'?"

"Well, in this case, a 'rider' simply converts the death benefit of the insurance policy into a long-term care payment. But if you don't use the entire amount of the long term care coverage, the remainder is passed to your heirs as a tax-free death benefit."

"Well that sounds pretty good. What you do you think Paul?"

"It does sounds very good."

Jack looked over at Linda and Paul with a smile, "Mark has never steered us wrong before, and it seems like a great idea... *to protect my inheritance.*" Jack chuckled a bit.

"So what would be the next steps if we decided that we wanted to buy the policies?" asked Linda.

"Well, the next step is to submit the applications, and get you both approved for the life insurance and the long-term care. There is no risk in applying, and once approved, we will know the actual costs for the life insurance and the long-term care rider."

"What do you think Paul?" asked Linda.

Paul looked first at Linda, then over at me, "Well Mark, this sounds like a win-win. I see nothing but upside in applying. Let's do it."

"Okay. It shouldn't take more than twenty to thirty minutes to apply, and then you will need to complete an in-home medical exam to show you are both in good health."

"That we are!" said Linda.

"When would you like to do your medical exam?" I asked.

"Oh, probably tomorrow afternoon." Both Linda and Paul agreed.

"Great, we'll set it for then."

"Well Mark, you said you had 'two things.' What was the second one?" Linda asked.

"Well, this may take some explaining, but here it goes.

"I suspect that you spent the last thirty years paying off your mortgage, so you wouldn't have a payment when you retire. Is that correct?"

"Yes, that's right," Linda responded.

"And you want to pass your home to your kids?"

Both Linda and Paul nodded. "Well, yes."

"What I'm suggesting, is that you get a reverse mortgage as soon as possible—to help protect and grow your assets."

Looking shocked and eyes wide open, Paul quickly jumped in, "Look Mark, I don't want to sound rude. But, what are you talking about a reverse mortgage for? We don't need the extra income. I read your book about the banking industry, and now it seems you want us to lose our home to the bank when we die?"

"No Paul, that is not true. In fact, the opposite is true. I want you to use a reverse mortgage to pass a *larger* legacy to your heirs, and actually protect *more* of your assets."

Jack jumped in, "Alright Mark, normally I would throw

anyone else out of my office for making such a suggestion. But because you have helped Ellen and I so much over the years, we are willing to hear you out."

"Okay, let me explain. I noticed one of your goals, Linda, was to have a vacation home when you retire. Is that correct?"

"Yes. But we can't afford to buy one."

"Have you ever looked at any vacation homes?"

"Yes we have. We sometimes look at real estate magazines on the airplane to Hawaii. It helps pass the time. But we just dream about it, knowing that we will never be able to afford one. We don't want another mortgage payment."

"Did you guys ever find a home that you really loved?"

"Yes, we did. There is a home we both fell in love with in Palm Springs, and it was for sale for $350,000. The payment would just be too high on a vacation home."

"Well, here is my suggestion. Since your home is worth about one million dollars, take a lump sum of $350,000 from your home using a reverse mortgage, and pay cash for the vacation home. Then you will own both homes, and have no payment on either."

Jack, Linda and Paul all looked a little stunned. There was a long silence in the room. I could almost hear Jack's wheels turning as he began to think through all the possible outcomes.

Finally, after a good couple minutes, Jack responded, "Well Mark, in over thirty years of being a CPA, I've never heard of this strategy before. It actually sounds pretty good. What's the catch?"

"There is no catch. All I need to show you is how to 'hedge' the reverse mortgage. We will make sure you have a much larger legacy than just one paid off home.

"How are you going to 'hedge' it Mark?" Jack asked.

"First, we must dispel some inaccurate information that many people believe about reverse mortgages. Most people believe that the bank takes your home after you die, leaving nothing to your heirs. That is simply not true. Reverse mortgages even go by a new name, specifically because of people's negative reaction to the words 'reverse mortgage.'

"Today, most reverse mortgages are known as Home Equity Conversion Mortgages, or 'HECMs.' It is true that the balance of a HECM mortgage must be paid off when you die, but that is also true of a regular mortgage. In both cases, when you pass your home to your heirs, whatever balance you have on the mortgage must be paid off. And, any equity that remains transfers to your heirs. The only difference is that with my plan, you will be passing the equity of two homes to your heirs rather than one."

"Two homes sound better than one." Linda smiled.

"Plus, you can even put your vacation home on 'Airbnb' when you are not using it—and collect rent to increase your retirement income. And Jack, being a CPA, will tell you that the rents collected can be tax-free due to the depreciation on rental property."

We again sat in silence. Jack, Linda and Paul seemed to be deep in thought.

After a minute, Jack spoke up, "Mark, I have to say, I think you are a genius. That is brilliant."

"Thanks Jack. I like this strategy so much, that if at age 40 I could qualify for a HECM mortgage, I would use one. I would invest what I was paying toward my mortgage and buy a second property. I would then rent the second property to create extra income.

"It would accelerate my plan for wealth-accumulation, and provide me a tax-free income stream. But unfortunately, my age alone would disqualify me. So I will have to wait until I'm 62."

"Like I said Mark, that is brilliant. You sure do think outside the box." Jack said.

"But that is not all. I've got a plan for you to pass on even more wealth, all completely tax-free. Do you want to hear it?"

"More wealth? And tax-free?" Linda had a big smile this time. "I like the sound of that. What is it?"

"Well, here is what we are going to do. Because you don't need all the rent you will collect from your vacation property, what we are going to do is take a portion of the rent and buy you what is called a 'second-to-die' life insurance policy."

"Second-to-die? What's that?" Linda asked.

"A second-to-die life insurance policy is designed for estate planning purposes. It only pays out after both you and Paul die. It is generally used to pass on tax-free wealth to your heirs."

"That sounds interesting."

"My plan is that we take $1,000 a month out of the rent you will be receiving to fund the life insurance policy."

"How much additional life insurance would it pass to our heirs?" Linda asked.

"Well, give me a minute, and I'll check." I pulled out my laptop and began to crunch some numbers.

"Assuming you are both in reasonably good health, we can get you a life insurance policy for $750,000."

Linda took a deep breath, "Let me get this straight Mark. We will pass on an *additional* $750,000 to our heirs, *plus* the appreciation on *two* homes rather than one, not have *any* mortgage payment on either properties, *and* our life insurance and long-term care will be paid for with the income from the vacation home?"

"Yup, that sounds exactly right Linda.

116

"And whatever balance is owed on the reverse mortgage when you pass away can easily be paid off with the $750,000 death benefit.

"But you want to know the coolest part of my plan?"

Linda looked really interested, "Of course I do!"

"Well, because the depreciation on the vacation home will offset the income you will receive from the rents, you will not pay any taxes when you *earn* the money. You will also not pay any taxes when you fund your life insurance policy. The policy cash value will grow with no taxes. And when you both die, you will transfer the $750,000 of life insurance tax-free."

"So when do we pay the taxes?" Linda asked.

Jack jumped in, "You don't Mom. You will never have to pay any taxes. That is what makes this plan so genius!

"It eliminates all the taxes. It passes on more wealth, and even reduces taxes when you die. And all you are doing is safely leveraging the *lazy* equity in your home.

"In fact, all my wealthy clients talk about how they use 'leverage.' They call it OPM.

"Mark, I've been a CPA for over thirty years, I've met with hundreds of different advisors, and I've never seen such creativity to pass wealth to heirs before. How did you come up with this?" asked Jack.

"Well, people tell me that I've always been an out-of-the-box thinker. I think that is the reason why I dropped out of college. I didn't want to be told *what* to think. I knew I would follow a different path since I wanted to become wealthy, and college was only teaching me to go get a job.

"I have been studying all aspects of finances for over 19 years, and I've also seen all the strategies that the other advisors recommend. And I realized that those strategies would, at best, leave their clients middle class. So today I only suggest strategies that can truly help my clients build wealth. And yes, I've done a fair amount of research on tax avoidance too."

"Well Mark, what would be our next steps?" Linda asked.

"Both you and Paul must do a phone interview before you can apply for a reverse mortgage. The government regulates reverse mortgages and they want to make sure you fully understand the advantages, and the disadvantages of it.

"Next, you must also get approved for a second-to-die life insurance policy. My staff and I can walk you through the whole process step by step. You know, baby steps.

"Now, I must let you know that I'm now running a bit late for my next meeting, so I have to go. But I'll have a mortgage broker that understands this strategy give you a call, and I'll have a Realtor that I trust also give you a call. Is that okay?"

"Sure, sounds good to me." Linda was beaming with joy.

"Because I don't have time today, I'll have my staff prepare the paperwork and call you to apply for the life insurance policy. I'll pop by later this week and have you e-sign it, and submit it right away."

Linda spoke up, "Well Mark, Jack is a CPA, and he will be getting a large chunk of our inheritance anyway, so I only have one question for you… *When do we start shopping for that vacation home?*"

Jack, Linda and Paul were all smiling when I left the office. I shook Jack's hand, and then Paul's, and Linda gave me a hug.

I was also smiling. I knew I had changed the family legacy of Linda and Paul, and Jack and Ellen forever.

If you would like more information on a HECM/ Reverse Mortgage, or a "Principal First Mortgage," text the word "mortgage" to: (833) 455-4540 **or Email:** 10ways@REMiiGroup.com

"One thing is clear: The Founding Fathers never intended a nation where citizens would pay nearly half of everything they earn to the government."
—Ron Paul

In Conclusion

"**Y**OU CAN'T AVOID TAXES—YOU'LL GO TO JAIL!"
I've heard those words many times, but only from those in the 99%.

What most Americans do not understand is the difference between tax *evasion* and tax *avoidance*. Tax evasion is illegal and you will likely go to jail, where tax avoidance is *completely* legal, and is the reason why the top 1% *are* "the Top 1%."

Unfortunately, this priceless information is almost exclusively taught only in the wealthiest of neighborhoods, when the rich teach their kids about money. And without a full understanding of this subject, it is highly unlikely you will ever join them.

It is true that you can't avoid *all* taxes. But as the Morgan Stanley advertisement stated, "You must pay taxes. But there's no law that says you have to leave a tip."

What I have learned is that those in the 99% use the word *can't* all the time.

"You can't avoid taxes…"

"You can't do this…"

"You can't do that…"

Or, "You can't get wealthy. You are the son of a bricklayer."

I've always ignored the advice of "can't do" people.

When people say "You can't do that," what they are really saying is, "I don't believe I can do it, so I don't want you to try either."

When *you* use the word "can't," you will always be right. Your brain immediately stops working on solutions to the problem. And with 100% certainty, you will *never* find the solution.

This is true for everything you believe you can't do… but also for the things you believe you *can* do.

About 19 years ago, when I was buried in credit card debt and student loans and working as a security guard for $8 an hour, I decided to eliminate the word "can't" from my vocabulary. I suggest you do the same, *if* you want any level of success in any area of your life.

Instead of using the word "can't," I choose to ask the question, "How can I do that?"

The question, "How can I do that?" is very powerful. It forces your brain to start working on solutions to your problem.

Have you ever had a problem that you have been thinking about when you go to bed, and when you wake up, you had *magically* found the solution?

How did that happen?

It *only* happened because you asked the question, "How can I (fill in the blank)?"

Now I have an important question for you before we end this book:

Right now, are you happy where you stand financially?

I'll assume your answer is "No," or "There's always more to learn"—otherwise you would have never picked up this book in the first place.

I'll also assume that you are in one of three demographics:

» Perhaps you are like me many years ago, when I was just starting to learn the basics of how money works.

» Or, you are in the middle class. And you are learning that the wealthy are using very different strategies than what you have been taught to do.

» Or perhaps you have already joined the top 1%, and are in search of more tax avoidance and wealth-accumulation strategies.

I hope you *all* have found the strategies in this book invaluable.

This book is an invitation for you to join the Top 1%, and beyond.

Are you coming along for the ride?

**If you work in real estate, mortgages, or tax
preparation and would like to add tax avoidance
strategies to your business,
text "Affiliate" to:** (833) 455-4540
or Email: 10ways@REMiiGroup.com

Congratulations!

YOU NOW HAVE ALL THE INFORMATION NEEDED TO avoid huge amounts of taxes on your road to building wealth. But there is one more important step: You may need to upgrade your current advisors.

A wealthy mentor once told me:

"Mark, if you want to get wealthy, you need to build a team. Your team should consist of financial professionals that are both specialists in their field, and understand all your specific strategies for tax avoidance and wealth accumulation. If one of your advisors doesn't fully support your goals, or they say 'that sounds too good to be true,' here is what I suggest you do: **find another advisor!**"

I'm passing this same advice on to you.

As I have increased my income, and my net worth, I have constantly added advisors that specialize in different strategies. I would not be where I am today financially—and would not have written two books—if it were not for following his advice.

Cheers!

GLOSSARY

Glossary of Financial Terms

After-tax money: Money that can be invested, after you paid your taxes on it.

Appreciation: An increase in the value of property or another asset.

Bond: A bond acts like a loan or an IOU that is issued by a corporation, municipality, or the U.S. government. The issuer (a corporation, municipality, or the government) promises to repay the full amount of the loan back to the bondholders on a specific date, plus pay interest for the use of the money.

Capital Gain: The difference between a security's (most commonly a stock or bond or real estate) purchase price and its selling price, when the price has risen.

Capital Gains Taxes (short term): The difference between an asset's purchase price and selling price (when the difference is positive) if sold prior to one year.
As of 2018, this is the same as ordinary income and is the highest form of taxes.

Capital Gains Taxes (long term): The difference between an asset's purchase price and selling price (when the difference is positive) if held for *more* than one year.

Historically this has been much less than ordinary income taxes.

Certificate of Deposit: Also known as a CD. The money is given to the bank, and they issue a promissory note. It earns an interest rate that is generally higher than the rate paid on savings accounts. The CD cannot be withdrawn until a specified date. If withdrawn prior to that date, a penalty can be charged from the bank (or credit union) for the early withdrawal.

Certified Public Accountant: An accountant who has met certain standards, including experience, age, licensing, and passed an exam in a particular state. They act as consultants on many issues, including taxes and accounting. A CPA helps individuals, businesses, and other organizations plan, reduce and avoid taxes.

Deprecation: From an accountant's perspective (and the IRS's), this is a gradual reduction in the value of an asset; such as a chair or computer in a business. This provides a tax-write-off, and reduces the amount of money earned, therefore reducing the taxes owed.

Depreciation is sometimes called a "phantom expense," or "phantom loss" when it pertains to real estate, as the value of the real estate can be going up, but on paper, it is "going down" in value. This offsets the income received from tenants.

Dividend: A distribution of earnings of those that own stocks or bonds. Dividends are usually paid monthly as cash, and are taxed at income tax rates. Municipal bond dividends can be exempt from taxes.

Enrolled Agent: A person who has earned the privilege of representing taxpayers before the Internal Revenue Service by either passing a three-part comprehensive IRS test covering individual and business tax returns, or through experience as a former IRS employee.

Exchange Traded Fund: Also known as "ETF," it is very similar to a mutual fund in that it (generally) invests in hundreds of stocks and bonds to reduce risk, and can be traded in the day like stock. Because ETF's don't have a money manager, the expenses are generally less than a mutual fund.

$250k/500k Home Sale Exemption: When you sell your home, the capital gains that would be due on the sale are waived, eliminating all the taxes.

Based on the Taxpayer Relief Act of 1997, if you are single you will pay no capital gains taxes on the first $250,000 of profit when you sell your primary residence. Married couples get up to a $500,000 exemption.

There are, however, some restrictions on this exemption. The home must be your primary residence for "two of the last five years" to qualify for the exemption. This exemption can be used every two years.

Income Taxes: A tax on a person's individual income from wages, gambling winnings, and other sources. These taxes are paid to fund the government and are also called a progressive tax. Progressive taxes go "progressively" higher as your income rises. There are both state and federal income taxes.

Indexed Universal Life Insurance: This is a type of life insurance policy where you can invest your after-tax money and grow it in a tax-deferred account. The money, called the "cash value," grows based on the performance of an index (such as the S&P 500), but is not actually invested in the market.

» IULs have a "floor" where you cannot lose any money even in a stock market decline.
» Most IULs have a "cap" which determines the maximum gain you can earn during a specific period. Some IULs today have "no capped" strategies.
» The money in this account can be used at any age and for any purpose, including funding college, or providing supplemental retirement income.
» You can add other basic coverage to the life insurance, such as long-term care, called a "rider."
» When you pass away, the death benefit, plus the cash value is passed to your heirs tax-free.

Individual Retirement Account (IRA): A retirement account that may be established by an employed person. IRA contributions are tax deductible according to certain guidelines, and the gains are not taxed until withdrawn after age 59 ½.

Inflation: A rise in the prices of goods and services, often equated with loss of purchasing power.

Interest rate: The fixed (or variable) amount of interest that a corporation, bank or government charges when borrowing or lending money.

IRC Code 7702 (and 7702A): Internal Revenue Code (IRC) Section 7702 defines what the federal government considers to be a life insurance contract, and how they're taxed. Section 7702A imposes limitations on the amount that can be invested into a life insurance contract each year, based on the size of the death benefit. It applies to life insurance contracts issued after 1985.

Liquidity: This describes the degree to which an investment can be quickly bought or sold in the market.

Long-Term Care: Also known as "LTC," involves a variety of services designed to meet a person's health or personal care needs during a short or long period of time. These services help people live as independently and safely as possible when they can no longer perform everyday activities on their own.

Long term care is a form of "asset protection" as it provides income to pay caregivers, rather than having to liquidate assets such as retirement accounts or a home.

Market-linked CD: Also referred to as an equity-linked CD, market-indexed CD, or an indexed CD. It is a specific type of CD that is linked to the performance of a stock or index, such as the S&P 500. Market-Linked CDs have market participation, but are guaranteed not to lose money.

Mutual Fund: Money that is (generally) invested in hundreds of stocks and bonds to reduce the risk. Mutual funds also have a money manager that may buy or sell stocks *within* the fund. Mutual fund companies report the performance of the fund at the end of the day, as opposed to an ETF which trades in the day, similar to a stock.

Municipal Bond (muni bond): State and local governments offer municipal bonds to pay for special projects, such as highways or bridges. The owners of the bonds, called "bondholders" receive interest for lending the money to the municipality. The interest that the bondholders receive is exempt from most, and sometimes all, income taxes.

Other People's Money (OPM): A common expression used when talking about the multiplying effect of using borrowed funds to purchase property rather than paying all cash.

Portfolio: A collection of investments owned by one organization or individual.

Probate: Is the judicial process whereby a will is "proved" in a court and is accepted as a valid public document that is the true last testament of the deceased.

The granting of probate is the first step in the legal process of administering the estate of a deceased person, resolving all claims and distributing the deceased person's property under a will.

Residual income: Residual income, also called "passive income," is income received on a regular basis, with little effort required to maintain it.

Reverse Mortgage, or "HECM" Mortgage: A loan borrowed against the value of one's home. The borrower (and their spouse) make no payments on the loan, and can live in the house for the rest of their life, regardless of the value of the home. When the borrower(s) die, the house is either sold and the value of the loan must be re-paid, or the beneficiaries have the option of refinancing the loan to a traditional mortgage.

To get a reverse mortgage, the homeowners must be at least 62 years of age and have 50% equity in their home. A home can also be purchased using a "HECM" loan, which would require 50% down on the property.

Roth IRA: A retirement account that may be established by an employed person. Roth IRA's are funded with after-tax money and they grow tax-free and can be withdrawn tax-free at retirement age.

Roth 401(k): In 2006, the government instituted a "Roth 401(k)" that allows paying the taxes now on the money being invested to have tax-free contributions at retirement, similar to a Roth IRA. A Roth 401(k) must be setup by an employer and has greater contribution limits than a Roth IRA.

Securities: Another name for investments, such as stocks or bonds.

Self-Employment Taxes: The taxes that are paid by business owners or those working as an independent contractor. In the United States, self-employed people pay double the social security taxes of employees, but are entitled to more tax deductions. Business owners and those self-employed use S-Corporations to reduce taxes, as corporations don't pay self-employment taxes.

Simplified Employee Pension IRA (SEP IRA): A SEP IRA is a variation of an IRA, and is used by business owners to reduce their taxable earnings and save for retirement.

Step-up in basis: Step-up in basis is the readjustment of the value of an appreciated asset for tax purposes upon inheritance, determined to be the higher market value of the asset at the time of inheritance.

When an asset is passed on to a beneficiary, its value is typically more than what it was when the original owner acquired it. The asset receives a step-up in basis so that the beneficiary's capital gains tax is minimized or eliminated.

Stock: A long-term, growth-oriented investment representing ownership in a company, also known as "equity."

Tax-loss harvesting: Tax-loss harvesting is the practice of selling a security (such as an ETF) that has experienced a loss. The sold security is replaced by a similar one, maintaining a very similar investment mix, and therefore a similar expected rate of return. By realizing, or "harvesting" a loss, investors are able to offset taxes on both gains and income.

Tax-loss harvesting has historically only been available to high net worth individuals.

Variable Universal Life Insurance: This is a type of life insurance policy where you can invest your after-tax money and grow it in a tax-deferred account. The money, called the "cash value," is invested in mutual funds, called "subaccounts."

» The cash value grows and declines based on the performance of the subaccounts.

» The money in this account can be used at any age and for any purpose, including funding college, or providing supplemental retirement income.

» You can add other basic coverage to the life insurance, such as long-term care, called a "rider."

» When you pass away, the death benefit, plus the cash value is passed to your heirs tax-free.

Zero Balance Account, or "Sweep Account": A Zero Balance Account (ZBA) is a checking account in which a balance of zero is maintained by automatically transferring all the funds from the account to somewhere else.

A ZBA is used by corporations and banks to eliminate excess balances in an account and move the money where they expect it to earn a higher rate of return.

401(k): 401(k) is a tax code, and is when an employee, and many times their employer, makes contributions into an investment to be used for the employee's retirement. It provides a tax deduction now, but both the growth and original money invested are taxed when distributions are taken in retirement. The distributions are taxed at both federal and state income tax rates.

With a 401(k), you can't touch your money until age 59 ½, otherwise a penalty applies, plus regular income tax rates.

15-Year Fixed Rate Mortgage: Also known as "15 year fixed loan," this type of loan has an interest rate that does not change over the life of the loan. It will pay off the loan in fifteen years. This loan carries a lower interest rate than a 30-year loan, but the monthly payments are higher.

30-Year Fixed Rate Mortgage: Also known as "30 year fixed loan," this type of loan has an interest rate that does not change over the life of the loan. It will pay off the loan in thirty years. This loan carries a higher interest rate than a 15-year loan, but the monthly payments are lower.

Made in United States
Orlando, FL
23 March 2024

45093041R00085